This book is dedicated to all the educators and students
who have influenced me in my journey.

Contents

Foreword

$\mathcal{I}$ first met Melinda when I went to Rome, Georgia, to deliver a workshop and she invited me to visit her school, the Floyd County Education Center. She told me that the school was composed of many students who had made bad decisions. Some had been adjudicated and had been given a choice of being expelled or going to her school. I agreed to visit, not knowing what to expect. When I arrived at the school, Melinda and members of her staff stood at the front door and welcomed every student. And every student, large and small, male and female, gave her a hug.

Anyone who has worked with Melinda recognizes that she is compassionate, articulate, intelligent, perceptive, and passionate about helping children and schools improve. *More Than a Test Score* demonstrates these concepts.

Melinda gives you, the reader, a comprehensive assessment as to what is currently taking place in education as well as a model for improvement. As she writes, "We must have the moral courage to look deeper than the symptoms of low academic achievement, high school dropouts, and teen pregnancy to examine the real root causes." And believe me, Melinda has the moral courage.

Educators have seen a dramatic increase in the number of at-risk learners, adjudicated students, students placed in special education, and school dropouts, and yet few have developed a process to reduce these factors. Many educators have given up on these students, writing them off. Not Melinda, her staff, or her school. This book describes a successful process.

The book is more than a "what to do" document; it is a "how to do it." Teachers, counselors, and administrators appreciate the "what to do" but need the "how to do it." The book is filled with specific techniques and resources and develops a clear roadmap easy for all to follow.

Melinda Strickland has not glossed over the difficulties of establishing a supportive learning environment. Her book is a call to action to those who wish to improve the state of education. I urge all who read it to go forth and do likewise.

Franklin P. Schargel
Albuquerque, NM

Acknowledgments

$\mathcal{W}$orking to fulfill a dream is never easy without the help and support of those around you. It is with heartfelt gratitude that I acknowledge my colleagues and family, whose help and support cannot be overlooked.

I never realized the value of growing up in the small town of Charleston, Tennessee, until I was off in college. Attending school in the same two buildings for grades 1 through 12 showed me the value of a small learning community and the influence of everyone involved in raising the children. It took me a long time to realize that not everyone was my "blood" kin, but everyone treated me as if they were. The teachers and staff encouraged me to do my best and not let obstacles prevent me from trying. The members of the community embraced me with life lessons and influenced me in many ways. Thank you, Charleston, for giving me wings!

To my mother, Lydia Atchley, you have been my personal prayer warrior and cheerleader throughout my life. You have always said I could do anything I set out to do.

To my terrific husband, Tim, you supported and encouraged me to seek my dream. As my soulmate, you walked this journey holding my hand each step of the way. On the days I couldn't do any more your love reached into my heart and revived my spirit.

To Meredith, Jake, Trevor, and Tylan, thank you for your support and understanding. Your support throughout this journey has amazed me. Thank you for the joys you create in my life each day.

To the staff at FCEC, your understanding and tireless effort is greatly appreciated. Thank you, Dr. Dale Hamby, Dr. Amy Allee, Dr. Rob Boice, Mrs. Kim Baker, Mr. Eric Burkhalter, Mr. John Bryant, Mr. Steve Buffington, Mr. Roger Dewey, Ms. Melissa Martin, Mrs. Sally Maddox, Mrs.

Jennifer Massey, Ms. Marisa Foster, Mrs. Laura Windom, Dr. Harvey Palmer, Mrs. Ann Talley, Ms. Lisa Nichols, Ms. Donna Johnson, Mrs. Faye Dawson, Mrs. Tanya Winston, and Mr. Jeff Bennett, for allowing me to share your ideas and going beyond all limits to help our students. Thanks especially to Dale and Amy, my critics and companions on this "project": without your support this would not be possible, nor near as much fun.

To the leaders and employees of the Floyd County school system, your support of our program has encouraged many students to stay in school and strive for a quality life through a quality education. Thank you for your encouragement by putting the needs of all students as the top priority in our system.

To all the students who have passed through the doors of the FCEC, you have taught me much more than I could ever teach you. Never settle for less than your best. It is time to rise above circumstances, continue to gain knowledge, and create your own success.

Thank you, Gracie and Rosie, for mentoring and encouraging me from day one in education by showing me the value of each child. You are invaluable and dear to me.

Finally, to my daddy, Claude Shell, you placed a high value on education all my life. You never let me settle for less than my best, even when I thought I had achieved it. Your guidance and assurance have made me the person I am today. I cannot begin to thank you for always, always showing me that I am responsible for what I become, and that you would always be there for me. Without your sacrifices each day, I would never have reached my dream. Thank you for making such a difference in my life.

Introduction

*T*ake a walk down memory lane to visit your years as a student. You may recall special events in school like fall festivals, dances, athletic events, or field trips. Don't forget your friends and times shared hanging out and having fun. When discussing school days almost every person can recall a special teacher who made an impact in his or her educational journey. That educator took the time to know all about you and challenged you to do your best. The teacher believed in your abilities and pushed you to excel. Your special educator developed a relationship with you.

Why am I driven to write a book about empowering at-risk students? In my 29 years as an educator, I have learned valuable lessons from those around me—especially from the students. The realization that students are people with desire, determination, and a future that depends on all of us is critical. These young adults have needs and wants that go beyond the walls of a school building.

This realization hit me during my early years as a classroom teacher of middle school students. The students in my seventh-grade class had worked hard to end the first semester and were eager to get home for the holidays. As usual, the students were excitedly sharing their plans and preparing for a muchneeded rest. As their teacher, I was determined to keep them focused on their mid-term exams and wrapping up the end of the term. I too wanted a rest and did not want to work over the holiday break.

Several of the students kept trying to get the rest of the class off task through normal chatter. These seventh graders were normal, everyday children who were too young to do some things and too old for others and really just had their own niche in society. Jamie was just like the others. He didn't fit in with his older siblings, but they watched over him and constantly

1

encouraged him to do well. Like his brothers, he was a talented athlete with a lot of potential and a strong desire to succeed. His mother was very supportive of his endeavors.

He could run very fast and had the stamina to run long distances. His grades were average, nothing near where they should be, and I had to prod him to answer a question in class. Most would say he was just a normal guy, shy around the opposite sex and focused on athletics and motorcycles. He did not make a point to be noticed in class; in fact, he just wanted to blend in with the others. Like them, he also had big plans for the holidays.

Only Jamie did not get to enjoy his holidays. After school Jamie was walking along the side of the highway and was struck by a car and killed. He was only 13 years old. Through Jamie's death I realized that the hopes, dreams, and future of this young man were gone in a matter of minutes. Everyone was devastated. The impact Jamie had made on all of us who knew him was not realized until his death. I had to painfully reflect on his role in my classroom.

Did he know the influence he had on his peers and teachers? Did I do my part to let him know the importance he played in my classroom? Or was he another student struggling through seventh grade to pass? My life was changed at that moment.

Upon returning to school after Jamie's death, I made a change. Academics were important, but so were the ambitions and dreams of the students. Caring for students as individuals and helping each one to know I was there behind each step of his or her journey became my priority. It has not changed in all my years as an educator.

This book is designed to focus attention on what is imperative in educating youth in today's society. The key element is caring for the whole child, not just academic learning. Educators need to take the time to build a relationship with the students and realize they have a need to be in control of what lies ahead for each one.

The focus of this book is giving the students power and control over their academic journey while instilling decision-making skills that will enable success long after they finish school. Strategies and techniques provided in this book have been effective with the at-risk students enrolled at our nontraditional school and can be easily adapted to any setting in any school. Classroom teachers have used these strategies to allow students to take ownership in making good decisions and improving their individual performance, which can enable the students to function effectively toward a successful future of their choice.

The strategies used in this book will help you find the right connection with youth in today's society by going outside the box, or better yet, simply throwing out the box that has driven education so strongly. Students need to be equipped to make appropriate choices that shape their lives. Self-esteem is not taught but is earned through responsible actions that enable students to learn by taking ownership in decisions. The image of many of today's youth is shaped by societal perceptions. Peer pressure is prevalent. Dealing with the stresses of everyday living has taken a toll on the morals and values of the youth.

Some of the information is research-based; however, much of it comes from the basics of reaching out to the students as individuals and changing the approach in working with these students. Meeting them where they are and providing the necessary survival skills works by reaching beyond the norms if educators have the right mindset. A variety of educational opportunities are available for students in need of a different approach to education. A one-size education fits no one when dealing with at-risk students. Many at-risk students arrive at school with a survival mindset rather than seeing the need for an education. How they will eat or where they will sleep at night, and whether an adult caretaker will be at home, take precedence over the need to learn.

The bottom line is this—the time to make a difference in the lives of students is now. The challenge is to recognize that our students are able to reach success, but not without direction. Not every child will grow up to graduate at the top of the class in college. Not every child will even go to college. The fact is every child can be the best in whatever path they choose by being smart. If one chooses to be a mechanic, then be the best mechanic ever.

The same goes if a child chooses to be a medical doctor: then be the best. This is accomplished by establishing and developing good work ethics, which include dependability, reliability, being on time and at work each day, and being dedicated to the job. Too many parents want to serve as their child's friend, lawyer, mediator, and banker instead of holding the child responsible for learning necessary life skills.

It is important for children to learn to handle disappointments and to be held accountable for choices they make while they are still under caring adult guidance. Constant support and communication are components for treating students as success stories who will thrive beyond their education years. Speak up and share the wealth of learning by discovering that the youth today are *more than a test score!*

The Power of the Test Score

It is possible to store the mind with a million facts and still be entirely uneducated.

—Alec Bourne

*D*oes intelligence make a person smart? Does being smart make a person intelligent? These two words are often used synonymously; however, they have two distinct meanings in relation to the education system and today's youth. Intelligence refers to knowledge gained through academic studies. Intelligence is measured through testing. Being smart is taking the intelligence given and applying it to maximize an individual's abilities and attributes in society.

For example, a person with average intelligence is smart when he takes that knowledge base and connects with a strong work ethic, positive life choices, and responsible attitude toward his future. He takes the intelligence and knows how to use it effectively.

The outcome of the American society, whether good or bad, is determined by the education of our students. Is the nation's education where it needs to be? Is the education system moving forward, encouraging our students to become successful, productive members of a society that incorporates principles based on a hard work ethic and caring for others? Are educators teaching today's students to become smart by using the intelligence they have acquired?

Students should have input into their educational journey. Students are not robotic beings programmed to be shuffled through the assembly line of the education system only to perform well on tests as present educational policies mandate. The products being shaped by schools should be more than test scores; they are individuals with futures depending on their overall performance

5

and choices. These students are the future leaders, parents, workers, and citizens of our society.

While tests and accountability are very important and critical in the education process, student achievement and outcome are based on far more than individual performance on tests. Students need to be empowered and held accountable for more than academic performance in education. What is going on with education in America depends on who is addressing the issue. Many politicians believe education in America today is holding educators and school systems accountable for producing quality learners.

The education system determines schools' success or failure based on test score criteria and schools' progress in meeting them. Educators may quickly respond to teachers who are not able to actively engage the students because of the demands of teaching high-stakes testing information. The test scores are the driving factor on the accountability status of the school; therefore, many educators are teaching the material that will be used on the tests.

Many parents share the idea that education is lacking because their children are not being taught responsibility or the life skills needed to make it in the real world. Students, on the other hand, would simply say they are being programmed to become efficient test takers regardless of knowledge and other achievements accomplished in their journey. Across the country students are complaining they have no time to discuss ideas or to solve problems because of the vast demand of assessment standards required (Lewis, 2006). The connection or relevance to real-world experiences is missing and seems unimportant to the education system and the lawmakers who are making educational decisions.

Education takes on new reform movements, often to improve student performance. When student performance levels are not where they should be, lawmakers create a new way of defining improvements. What is amazing about these various "reform" efforts is that nothing is being eliminated. Each reform brings new ideas and strategies for improving education, and yet nothing improves. New ways of educating the students are simply being added to the fold of the reorganization movements.

Piles and piles of reforms are being added, which places more demands on the students and the adults working with them. Dictated from the national level, changes trickle down to local systems, which decipher the protocol only to be held accountable for all aspects of the newest mode of reform. One of the biggest problems pertains to efforts among local systems to reinvent the educational reforms for their students. Local control is essential for meeting the educational needs of the students; however, data collection should be similar across the nation when comparisons are made.

Myles Friedman defines a variety of tests used in the educational system in his book *No School Left Behind*. He believes that many tests are used incorrectly. He states:

> Tests that try to serve the purposes of all educators may serve the purposes of none. Basing grades, promotions, and graduations on test results that are relative—that is, norm-referenced—is indefensible. National normed achievement tests may be useful in comparing the performance of groups and group members, but they cannot be used to judge individuals' achievement of class learning objectives.
>
> Worse, these tests are being used in ways that they were not designed for. To use one test score for admissions, placement, or any other kind of decision about an individual student is seriously misguided. Accountability testing is used to judge teachers and administrators as well as students. (Friedman, 2005, p. 94)

Tests used in American schools perform a different function. The variety of tests often is misinterpreted by the average adult. The tests are described in general terms without providing clear definitions for their purpose.

Friedman further indicates that multiple types of testing can help identify students' misgivings, weaknesses, or failures. This can help provide more diagnostic information to design more suitable instructional needs to help certain students learn according to their needs. In designing a test we must use adequate terminology that is relevant to education. Friedman relates that three important components to test include reliability, validity, and objectivity.

The decisive focus has been based on educational accountability of states and schools under the No Child Left Behind (NCLB) legislation signed by President Bush in 2002. NCLB contains the most sweeping overall changes in education since it replaced the Elementary and Secondary Education Act of 1965. Another federal education legislation called Goals 2000 was based on the theory of standards-based education reform. Formerly known as outcome-based education, it was grounded on the belief that high expectations and setting goals will result in student success for everyone.

These major reforms were the result of the "panic" mode initiated by *A Nation at Risk* back in 1983. The U.S. educational system was reprimanded for its failing results and for accepting mediocrity instead of excellence. The National Commission of Excellence in Education report, *A Nation at Risk*, demonstrated that competing countries were excelling in education advancement at a greater rate than American students. The goal was for the U.S. Department of Education to "tighten the reigns" on education and increase the standards. Administrators, teachers, parents, and students were to be held accountable through a more rigorous instructional program.

According to *Learning Curve*, published by the Urban Institute (2003), accountability is defined so that states must develop performance-based accountability systems, define and measure adequate year progress (AYP) for student performance, and apply sanctions to districts and schools that fail to meet AYP goals. The state accountability system must treat academic assessment as the primary indicator of performance. The law states that a secondary academic indicator, graduation rate, must also be measured. Safeguards are in place to prevent schools from pushing out lower-performing students. In other words, AYP cannot be met or exceeded based on dropout rates.

Dr. Jane Bluestein discusses the controversy about assessments in her book *Creating Emotionally Safe Schools* (2001). It is as critical to assess student performance as it is to use the testing to benefit the overall educational process. The value of assessment is undeniable for determining improvement areas in student understanding or helping with instructional strategies. To justify assessments as a motivational component changes the focus from the learning process to performance inadequacies. And this is where the road tends to get a little rocky. Bluestein further states:

> when the consequences begin to threaten students' promotion or graduation, educators' salaries and job security, district funding, schools' autonomy and even real-estate values, testing—specifically, high-stakes standardized testing—can become downright dangerous. (p. 89)

It is difficult to determine if the tests are productive. So much educational jargon is used to confirm data that shows that assessments are helpful; however, just as much confirms the other side of it all. Are the tests helping or hindering the students? Where does the chaos end? Are we serving students or having to justify education?

"Testing the Joy Out of Learning," written by Sharon Nichols and David Berliner (2008), relates how high-stakes testing is causing a problem for reluctant learners. Schools that promote testing as the "make or break" component for success are robbing students of their motivation to learn. The message is clear:

> High-stakes testing encourages teachers to view students not in terms of their potential, or what unique or new qualities they bring to the learning environment, but rather as test-score increasers or suppressors. Students quickly pick this up and realize they are defined as winners or losers on the basis of their test scores. (p. 15)

In the article "To See Beyond the Lesson," Jacqueline Brooks (2004) explains the controversies surrounding teaching. Her focus is on "teaching for meaning," giving students time to reflect and use critical-thinking skills. Teachers are not having the opportunities to engage students in significant problem-solving activities because of the strenuous curriculum. She states:

> Many educators and members of the general public think it is appropriate for students to complete worksheets of multiple-choice questions in preparation for a test. We will never channel productive energy into creating the schools we really want unless we give up the magical belief that test preparation is a suitable surrogate for education. (p. 9)

Since the state-mandated tests are so comprehensive, teachers are pressured to teach to the test in fear of losing their job. There is little time for flexibility or enrichment opportunities provided for the teachers. Rigorous schedules and material have to be covered or the teacher may be out of a job. It is sad when teachers, who have the love for helping the students, cannot even engage in classroom discussions to expand an idea. It is no wonder that students are becoming disengaged with education due to the shallow methods of teaching to the test.

Bill Milliken, founder of the Communities in Schools (CIS) program and author of the book *The Last Dropout* (2007), shares the importance of measuring more than how well students complete tests in school. What is needed is a way to validate and measure how well students succeed in more than just a classroom. He states, "systems weren't designed to show effectiveness; they were set up not to show ineffectiveness, and the positive gets covered up along with the negative. They not only cloud the bad news, they conceal the potential solution" (p. 169).

With each state establishing its own guidelines for measuring accountability and each school system using various data, how valid is the information anyway? The difficulty is trying to establish precedents for comparison when one district measures one item and another district measures something else but it is all labeled under the same criteria. The federal government collects the data and therefore determines an effective from an ineffective school based on different data.

The point is that testing is critical and important when put in the right perspective. Using tests to measure progress of a student can be an invaluable tool to identify areas for improvement or to assess skills. Testing scores are not the sole component that should be used to measure the success or failure of a school system or determine the success or failure of the American education system. Too much emphasis is being placed on testing without criteria that validate performance on an even playing field. This chapter has identified various perspectives of the testing dilemma and the frustration that is common due to the misuse of data.

KEY POINTS

- NCLB has put accountability of the education system in the forefront of assessing schools.
- AYP and graduation rate are indicators used to determine how well an educational system is performing.
- Each state has the leeway to determine how data is collected with approval from the U.S. Department of Education.
- Testing is critical and very important in assessing student progress in school.
- Testing has been defined in a variety of ways.
- Norm-referenced tests compare how well a student performs in comparison to a group of students.
- Criterion-referenced tests evaluate how well objectives are mastered.
- The problem lies within the power of the score and in basing the power of the score on what it really is.
- The testing issue is critical because of how the scores are used, not for the reality of testing student knowledge.
- Basing a student's future solely on test scores is wrong.
- Education is suffering due to teachers having to teach to the tests.
- Success in school is determined by more factors than just test scores.

• 2 •

MIA: Mission in Action
Service Learning

*Reading and writing, arithmetic and grammar do not constitute
education, any more than a knife, fork and spoon constitute a dinner.*

—John Lubbock

$\mathcal{E}$ducators working with at-risk students should have a variety of strategies for reaching these students. While academics are important to educators, other qualities are equally important for children to be successful in society. Creating compassionate, supportive, and responsible young adults enables students to become productive and caring citizens of tomorrow rather than robotic test examinees. While not every child will score exceedingly high on standardized exams or meet basic proficiency scores, every child can be great by helping others.

As an educator working with at-risk learners, I see the frustration level of the students that is readily visible in their performance in the classroom. Much of the frustration has stemmed from the lack of voice in their individual academic programs. Many schools allow students to choose elective courses such as art, band, chorus, and physical education; however, this does not satisfy the at-risk learner's need to belong. Stakeholders talk *about* the student but rarely *to* the student. It is a discouraging part of the educational process.

Tragically, today's educators are going through the motions of education by treating students as products. Life is filled with emotions, dreams, and the reality of everyday struggles. The questions that continue to haunt us today include: Are educators preparing our students to effectively use and incorporate academic knowledge and face the real world? Or is education simply providing data for students to process? Are teachers simply feeding information into the minds of students? The answers to these questions lie in the sad

11

reality that many educators are so pressured to meet the state accountability mandates placed on them in the schools.

Where do students learn to cope with and manage life's adversities? Some contend it is the parents' responsibility or perhaps religion's. Simply put, it is everyone's responsibility. We need to stop pointing fingers at each other and face the fact that all are responsible for creating learning environments where every student should be the focus of the attention. While politicians and business leaders are looking at the wrongs in American education, students are dropping out of school.

Students walk into our building believing they are just part of a system where adults are telling them what to do. The sad truth is they are correct. Educators are determined to make decisions based on what they believe to be best for the students; however, no one is listening to the students. Students need to be involved in their educational journey and take responsibility for choices made.

The at-risk student needs to see the value of academics and how the courses relate to everyday living. Making the personal connection of what is learned in school to what is expected of individuals in life after high school is a critical component for the learner. The lack of input shuts down the at-risk learners so they just go through the motions of learning. These students need the ability to connect with courses and instructors that enable participation and to share ideas and opinions as learning occurs. Relevance to real life is critical for at-risk learners to absorb academic information and connect it effectively.

True accountability is measured by how well students process the academic knowledge gained in school and use it effectively in the lives they lead. It is not necessarily how well they do on test scores.

The frustration levels created by the lack of connection, or relevance, of academics with real life are seen in various forms with the at-risk learner. They manifest in discipline problems, antisocial behavior, or simply shutting down. Students may drop out of school, become involved in gang activity, or enter the judicial system for various infractions.

Myles Friedman shares the following, taken from the book *No School Left Behind*:

> The goal of education is not to stuff children's heads with dates and formulas, but to prepare them to be useful, productive citizens. Well-educated students are those who know how to think critically, how to solve problems, how to work well collaboratively, and how to innovate. But children must want to learn what they are being taught; they must be active partners with their teachers. Students control what they are willing to learn. (Friedman, 2005, p. 69)

Effective educators are needed to help guide students' academic and behavioral success. Educators have long been in the pivotal position of providing for and meeting all needs of students. Motivating all students should be a focus for educators in order to help students be successful academically, behaviorally, and socially. This takes consistent research on curriculum and best practices.

Students learn best when an educator meets the students where they are and guides them in a positive direction. Doing this requires finding what works for the student and encouraging success through opportunities. No one set way will work for all students, so educators must get to know their students as individuals.

Making the connection of classroom learning to real-life experiences is a great tool to provide student success while providing the motivation needed for students to see the relevance of academic learning. To enhance student achievement and provide life-long skills, the strategy of service learning has been effectively utilized for several years. Improvements have been evident in students' academic skills, attendance, and behavior.

The MIA: Mission in Action service-learning program at the Floyd County Education Center (FCEC) was created as a dropout prevention strategy to increase social development, decrease inappropriate behavior, and provide a positive outlook on education. According to the National Dropout Prevention Center/Network, 15 strategies were developed by Dr. Jay Smink and Franklin Schargel to prevent at-risk students from dropping out of school. Of the 15, the FCEC's service-learning program encompasses 11 of these strategies.

This program was implemented to assist students in improving behavioral and social skills by providing volunteer services that connect academic learning to real-life experiences. Through service learning, students have the opportunity to improve life skills, support employment opportunities, establish self-discipline while working with peers, and increase awareness of needs among community members and agencies.

The MIA: Mission in Action service-learning program was fashioned as a way to assist students in improving behavioral and social skills, to empower students to be accountable for choices, and to make a difference through providing services to help others. Students are taught the importance of helping others everyday, not just on Make a Difference Day, Youth Service Day, and so on. Impressed upon the students is the importance of seeing others' needs and responding without recognition. Just do it because it is the right thing to do. Students are taught, no matter how bad they believe their current situation is, to look over their shoulder and realize someone else has it worse.

To measure success requires more than just test scores. Marty Duckenfield and Sam Drew (2006), of the National Dropout Prevention Center in Clemson, South Carolina, claim the current system of NCLB measures knowledge but fails to measure other important variables that matter. Other variables that boost learning and point toward whether a student will be successful in school and life as a productive member of society are not part of the accountability indicators of NCLB.

Success in school is determined by more factors than how well students perform on academic tests (Duckenfield and Drew, 2006). All that matters in school is not always measured. Important protective factors of education are found in research completed by the Minneapolis-based Search Institute. Students who possess fewer of the 40 "developmental assets for healthy youth development" are at a higher risk of dropping out of school than those who possess more. Some of the protective factors include support, empowerment, establishing boundaries and expectations, positive values, and a commitment to learning.

One of the key assumptions and principles of the *Growing to Greatness* 2006 initiative states, "Nearly all systematic collection of information on adolescents measures their deficits, not their positive participation in society" (Duckenfield and Drew, 2006, p. 3). Educators need to focus on teaching the love of learning and end results associated with becoming life-long learners. Building positive relationships with people around the students and learning to support endeavors are means to engaging students in school.

Duckenfield and Drew identify assets, other than academics, that a high school graduate should know. Educators agree that graduates should also:

- be productive citizens, workers, and family members who possess critical-thinking and problem-solving skills;
- be able to ask questions and research answers;
- have an ability to get along with others;
- possess the skills needed to work effectively on a team;
- possess good oral and written communication skills;
- become people who are engaged in their communities; and
- care about others. (p. 35)

Through a structured program, service learning lends a "helping hand" that is needed to change their negative mindset and show relationship and relevance to the curriculum. By helping others and becoming productive members of society, these students help themselves. The early years of service learning encompassed four major components: preparation, action, reflection, and celebration. This model is known as the PARC model and was designed by the Institute for Global Education and Service Learning. It worked well until students shared that they needed more input into the process and design of the service-learning program.

Through improvements the core of the MIA: Mission in Action service-learning program now follows the 10 steps defined by the Institute for Global Education and Service Learning, which include: (1) preparation or planning, (2) meaningful service, (3) reflection, (4) participant voice, (5) genuine need, (6) connection to learning, (7) diversity, (8) partnerships, (9) assessment, and (10) evaluation. Using these areas as the foundation enabled the expansion of a more meaningful program with defined parameters for completion. The students embraced the additional concepts, and the projects improved with more input and voice from the students.

The purpose of service learning is to blend service and learning so that service reinforces, improves, and strengthens the learning, and the learning reinforces, improves, and strengthens service. We want our student to learn the importance of making a difference to those around them. The experiences of our students who are involved in service-learning programs benefit not only the school but also the community and other young people. Service learning helps build community support and partnerships beyond school. Many projects are developed collaboratively with the community and the students.

A few years ago a neighbor across the street, Melvin Grogan, visited our school. Our school is located in one of the old school buildings in the Johnson/Model community. Melvin came to visit and wanted to find out about our program that was housed in his old school. You see, Melvin graduated from our school when it was Johnson School. He asked if his class could hold their 50-year reunion at the school. Our students embraced the idea and wanted to make it a special time for Melvin and his classmates. The students started collecting yearbooks, trophies, and other memorabilia from when Melvin and his classmates were in school.

Our students talked with people in the community and developed a history of the Johnson School years. They provided their collection to the alumni to have at their 50-year reunion. The students organized the set-up and learned so much about the community. Many alumni from out of town even came by for tours. This project enhanced a long-standing bond with the community. Melvin still talks about the great reunion as he keeps a close eye on our school. It was a great experience for everyone involved.

Service learning facilitates a closer bond between school, community, and home. Through community projects, parents are more easily drawn into the educational process. Service provides an easily accessible forum, which serves to encourage parental involvement in the education of their children.

Parents, who often feel alienated from the normal academic routine of school, find a more comfortable common ground where they can become actively involved. As a result, parents become part of the educational process and begin to share accountability for their children's education along with the school, thus strengthening the educational process.

Further, the community is benefited by service learning because students are endowed with a sense of civic efficacy, the attitude that they should, can, and will have an impact on civic affairs. Young people become more aware of the balance between rights and responsibilities as citizens of a democratic community, and as a result they are more likely to act upon this awareness in ways that benefit the local community, state, and nation. Many students discover a sense of meaning in education when they are able to examine firsthand the community's social problems or participate in the operations of the local government.

Service learning enables students to see the connection, or relevance, of education through direct experiences in the local community, and the process develops more positive attitudes toward school and education in general.

A PowerPoint orientation is presented to the students prior to the start of service learning. Students are taught the rationale and purpose of service learning and how to reflect on their service through a journal that features their experience. Each student is given a handbook with detailed explanations of the components, parent permission/student participation form, time sheet, self-assessment, and evaluation. Students complete an inventory of interests to help determine what areas would be the most meaningful to them.

Individual students are permitted to develop a proposal and complete an individual project that meets the criteria established by the staff at school. These criteria involve meeting the needs of others, absence of compensation, connection with one or more academic class, and safety. Each adult in the school is responsible for facilitating a service-learning group and overseeing activities associated with learning.

By completing projects, students gain a sense of belonging and self-worth and establish good community relationships. Students connect the relevance of education and put academic knowledge into meaningful practice while gaining ownership of and responsibility toward helping the community. The students and facilitators develop a unique relationship by working together, sharing ideas, and creating an effective plan to implement the projects. Attitudes toward school change, creating a positive environment with a sense of belonging for students.

Through a Learn and Serve grant in 2005, the FCEC received funding to implement the various service activities. Before receiving the grant, many projects were funded through community donations, teachers' personal funds, and a partnership with CIS. Tools and equipment were brought from home by faculty members and parents of students. The Learn and Serve grant provided funds to support the program and give students access to technology-related activities that expanded service-learning opportunities.

GETTING STARTED

To initiate a service-learning program it is crucial to gain insight and support from stakeholders who will participate in the program. The following steps may help in developing a starting point to an effective plan:

1. Decide who will participate in the project. For example, one small group may choose to complete one project, or several groups may do several projects. It may be best to start small and expand as you go.
2. Survey the participants to see what kind of project interests them. Some participants may prefer to be physically involved while others may choose to be behind the scenes. Physical involvement may include building projects, serving food at a soup kitchen, or cleaning up a park. Participants behind the scenes may choose to write letters to troops, make brochures with important information, or create posters, for instance.
3. Have the participants research the needs in your community. What is going on that interests them? This is a great time to look at the local newspapers and community flyers. Someone may have had personal experience with a friend, relative, or peer who faced a disease or personal calamity and may convince the others to work for a cause. Examples may include cancer, diabetes, or organ donation. For younger participants, the adult facilitator may need to bring ideas to the group. It is critical that all participants be allowed to have a voice in the process.
4. Project selection. The participants will select a project to complete. This can be done by majority vote or presentations by individuals. The participants will decide on one project or may map out a plan to include several projects over a period of time.
5. Define each participant's role. One should serve as the chairman who will lead the group. A cochairman will help with the leadership and serve as chairman when necessary. Another participant should serve as the recorder to keep up with the recording of minutes and order of activities. Other participants may be given specific roles or serve as the remainder of the group in helping with the project.

6. The adult facilitator is the key to creating the learning environment and connecting the service-learning project to academics. The facilitator takes care of getting approval for the project and collecting permission forms, volunteers, and reflection of the activities associated with the project.

Synopses of a few service-learning projects completed at the FCEC are given. The students are the leaders, have various roles within their chosen group, and are selected by a consensus of the group members.

ANGEL EXPRESS

This MIA: Mission in Action service-learning group works with Angel Express. Angel Express is a nonprofit charity organization founded by a true angel, Mrs. Janet Baltzer. Mrs. Baltzer created Angel Express in 1994 as a way to help those in need. Angel Express has been housed in the FCEC for the past several years. The mission of the group is to help those in need, always respecting individuals of diverse cultures. The organization has collaborated with over 60 local social service agencies, successfully brightened over 22,000 Christmases, sponsored dozens of year-round holiday and literacy events, and provided countless opportunities for community service.

Angel Express is an all-volunteer organization. Mrs. Baltzer and her volunteers have embraced the FCEC students and included them in various activities for others. Activities include a party for the special education students at Johnson Elementary once a semester. The FCEC students are involved in planning the party, helping decorate, preparing goody bags, and interacting one on one with the students during the party.

Countless students have made tremendous strides in their lives by helping those around them. Jeremy was a student at our school who had a negative attitude toward everything. He was assigned to our program because of defiance of authority and continuous disruption that prevented others around him from learning. He was belligerent toward all adults and believed the world owed him something. His bullying demeanor kept everyone at a distance. He wanted those who cared about him to leave him alone and let him do what he wanted, when he wanted. He was receiving counseling and other anger-management programs to help him combat his disruptive behaviors.

Jeremy did what he wanted to do no matter what the consequences. He was capable of making good grades; however, he believed people would see him as a "nerd" or a weak individual who was easy to pick on. He tried his best to shut everyone out. Our teachers worked hard to break through the tough outer shell and reach in to find the real Jeremy.

It was during his second assignment to our program and with his mother's consistent help that reality hit Jeremy. He was working with one of the service-learning groups but was removed because of his behavior. I placed him with the Angel Express group because they were having a party for a group of elementary special-needs children. My reasoning behind the move was that a party was uplifting and fun to most students. Jeremy liked the attention that he received when around a group of people.

One of the special-needs students who attended the party was visually impaired. In fact, he was blind and would not separate himself from his paraprofessional, or aide. He had visited our campus with his classmates on several occasions and would never really involve himself with the parties unless his teacher or paraprofessional was at his side.

Because of the beautiful spring weather, the party was held outside in our commons area. This enabled the students to participate in jumping rope, playing with hula hoops, drawing on the sidewalk, and many more fun outdoor activities. The service-learning group provided assistance to supervise the games and activities.

Jeremy noticed the visually impaired student standing alone in the room. He befriended him and before long was escorting him around to the various groups. Jeremy stayed with the student the entire party and seemed to enjoy himself. Of course, the paraprofessional was close at hand; however, the visually impaired student didn't seem to notice. He and Jeremy had a blast.

After the service-learning activity was completed, Jeremy came and shared his experience with me. I was stunned to find Jeremy's compassion and excitement over helping a younger student. With big eyes and a smile, Jeremy kept saying, "He liked me, he really liked me!" It took all I had to hold back tears of joy upon seeing the expression on Jeremy's face. Not only did his attitude toward others change, so did his attitude toward himself. Jeremy completed his assignment at the alternative school, enrolled in the Youth Challenge program, and received many honors and awards for his service and physical activities. What a difference Jeremy made!

The group also creates goody bags for the AIDS Resource Council, the clients of Network Day Services, and various other organizations serving the needy of Rome and Floyd County. During fall semester, members prepare for the toy giveaway hosted by Angel Express by putting together, sanding, painting, and decorating baby beds with the help of community volunteers. The members also help with organizing the toys for distribution. The toy giveaway unites various organizations throughout North Georgia that provide toys at Christmas time for those in need.

WOODSTOCK

The Woodstock MIA group makes Adirondack chairs. A retired member of the community volunteers to help with this project, guiding the students to create a project that promotes relaxation and outdoor enjoyment. Members of the group work toward developing team-building activities through construction, managing costs, and sales while also addressing outdoor environmental issues. Money generated from the sales is donated to the Pulmonary Hypertension Association. Sally Maddox, a math teacher at the FCEC, has been diagnosed with pulmonary arterial hypertension (PAH) since 1990. When she was diagnosed there was no treatment for PAH, and she started on calcium channel blockers. Back then, patients were immediately listed for a lung transplant. For the past 11 years, she has run a support group for patients with PAH, their caregivers, and medical professionals who deal with the disease. She has also served on the board of directors of the Pulmonary Hypertension Association for the past 10 years. For the past five years, she has planned the annual Fun Walk for a Cure, and to date the walks have raised over $50,000. Collected monies are used for patient support services and research projects. There are currently six treatments approved by the FDA for treatment of PAH. Mrs. Maddox is currently on two of those new treatments, is inactive on the transplant list, and is doing well.

The students in the group elected to help raise money for the PAH group to rally support and enhance the research for PAH. Not only did the students build and sell Adirondack chairs, but members of the group also researched this disease and provided information to be used by the foundation. Students discovered the difficulties faced by Mrs. Maddox and experienced firsthand what helping was all about.

FCEC N.E.W.S. (NORTH EAST WEST SOUTH)

The goal of this group is to provide information to the WebCrawlers website group, establish news releases to inform the community about the positive aspects of FCEC, promote community involvement, and acquire grant information for service learning.

The N.E.W.S. service-learning group builds community support and a better understanding of nontraditional education, takes pictures of all activities, interviews and writes press releases about participants in all service-learning groups, posts information on the website, and submits articles to the local newspaper.

First, there is a need to change the perception of the academic and behavioral processes at FCEC. The perception of the community is that the nontraditional school is for bad students. Next, the group will point out the need for public education to help students develop a sense of problem solving, decision making, creative thinking, goal setting, and self-control to enhance academic learning.

Victoria ("Vic") was assigned to our program because of getting into fights throughout her high school. She was a very angry young lady and often held grudges against others without provocation. During the initial stages of deciding which group to work with, Vic stated that she was interested in the media. Vic, a senior, became passionate about this project when she realized that she had great communication skills, especially in interviewing others.

Vic discovered her leadership abilities when she was called on by the group to serve as the chairman. She began leading the meeting and making assignments to the other members. Vic's confidence soared as she realized her self-control, and her anger became less evident. She worked diligently reporting on the flood of issues associated with poverty and especially with the needs of dysfunctional families. Her research and skills led her to realize that regardless of race, gender, or income level all individuals were the same. Vic even discussed the possibility of studying journalism in college and becoming a reporter.

<hr />

HABITS OF THE HEART

The students in the Habits of the Heart service-learning group made "Blessing Bears" to be donated to local agencies. The Blessing Bears are small stuffed bears that bear a message to the recipient and bring a blessing when hugged. The goal of the project was to communicate to people in need and make their day better because others care. Blessing Bears were distributed to heart surgery recovery patients, nursing home patients, and children recovering in hospitals.

The students were guided by a volunteer, Lydia Atchley from Cleveland, Tennessee, who taught them the process of completing this project. From making the pattern, sewing the fabric, stuffing the bears, to adding the finishing touches, she walked them through to the end. Many of the students had never sewed anything using a needle and thread, much less a sewing machine.

This activity provided many life and career-building skills that enabled students to step out of the box of normalcy and create a lasting impression on the maker and the recipient.

Tony was a middle school student who was sent to us because of fighting issues. His father was not in his life, and this caused many anger issues that surfaced in his middle school years. Tony would not involve himself in anything to redirect his anger or release the pent-up energy. His mother tried to find activities to help him.

Tony immersed his energy in working with the Blessing Bears during the project time. He worked diligently cutting out the patterns and learning how to use the sewing machine. It was really amazing to see him develop a sewing talent in such a short time. He successfully completed several bears but also realized his ability to redirect his energies and led the group to name each bear.

Tony's attitude changed, and his success in this project helped him to realize that he was responsible for his future. Taking opportunities to make something for others was a plus and made him feel better about himself. He was instrumental in presenting the bears to the organizations and realized the need to help.

***

COVERING THE COMMUNITY

Covering the Community is an ongoing clothes closet project in which members collect, sort, and distribute clothing items to those in need. This group researched the poverty levels in the community and discovered a need for a clothing closet to help people in need. Located on the school campus, the clothes closet is available throughout the school year to organizations, school social workers, churches, or anyone in need. The community utilizes this service for various reasons, including emergencies such as house fires, displacement, poverty, or disaster situations. Ms. Donna Johnson, a paraprofessional at the FCEC, facilitates this project with the students in multiple classrooms throughout their assignment.

Recently a flood occurred in a surrounding county. Using the opportunity to help, the students in the science classroom studied the flood's impacts, such as water damage, germs, and soil changes, that affect the community. Homes, churches, and schools were flooded and left many students and families without clothing. Our students and facilitators made a plea to the community to drop off clothing for the victims. Over two truckloads of clothing were delivered with the help of community volunteers to transport the items.

The students have collected clothes and organized them in an empty classroom. They have had to establish parameters and create a brochure with the guidelines for acceptable clothing. The students are responsible for gathering and sorting the clothing to fill the requests made by the community. Appointed pick-up times are set, and an inventory of items is kept.

Many of the students who work in this group are also in need of clothes. To keep the true faith of service learning, students are allowed to bring in clothing items and swap them for items in the clothes closet. If there is a true need for students at the school, the social worker is contacted, and clothing is arranged with the parent or guardian without the student's knowledge.

⸰⸰⸰

WEBCRAWLERS

By using the Netchalk website creator program, this group of students helps to maintain the school website by collecting information and reviewing and editing material that is presented by stakeholders for submission. The Web-Crawlers are also involved with responsibilities for other community websites, such as the Turning Point site through the sheriff's department. This brings academics into today's system of communication and promotes technology skills at various levels. It provides career-building skills that enhance communication and teamwork that will enable success in the future.

Postings from all MIA: Mission in Action groups as well as school and community events are maintained and updated by this group of technology-oriented students. The WebCrawler group experiences firsthand the benefits of using a great communication tool for showing off the school and student achievements.

Kenny was assigned to finish his high school career at the nontraditional school during his junior year. A natural on the computer, Kenny signed up to work with the WebCrawlers and immediately found his calling. He embraced the activities associated with working on the web page and often came in with new ideas or "the latest" techniques of web page design. Very few days passed that Kenny did not rush into school with a list of web pages that he found to have unique characteristics that would work with the program. He even found a job working with a company on web page designs. Pages of research and ideas were presented to everyone who would listen to him. Kenny would work after school and during any minute of free time to come up with new ideas or tweak his latest innovations.

Kenny graduated several years ago and continued working for the web page design company. Recently, Kenny bought the company and is now the owner. He found his place to belong and make a difference for others with his passion for technology.

—⸗—

WAM (WE ARE MEN)

Only a man who knows what it is like to be defeated can reach down to the bottom of his soul and come up with the extra ounce of power it takes to win when the match is even.

—Muhammad Ali

What does it take to be a man? WAM was created to guide young males in understanding what it means to be a man. In today's world of conflicting definitions and expectations, it is only fair that we equip our young people with the tools necessary to grow into the people they want to become. Many of the students in this group have no strong male influence in their life, or they have a desire to become better men in today's society.

WAM is a voluntary program that accepts students who are willing to stand up for what they believe and go the extra mile to develop characteristics and essential skills for the responsibilities they will face in their future as they grow older and begin to make choices that not only impact their lives but the lives of others in society.

Some of the characteristics WAM will be targeting are:

Physical	Functional	Sense of Adventure
Sexual	Emotional	Honor
Intellectual	Interpersonal	Respect
Ambition	Pride	
Honesty	Competitiveness	

Of course, the characteristics of a man are not limited to the above, but these are certainly foundational. Each young male will look at his strengths and weaknesses and begin to develop his own sense of who he wants to be, not who or what others say he should be. Members of the community (even former students) are involved in helping develop the essentials of this project. Mentorship is a part of WAM, so anyone who is a positive role model to these students is welcome to participate.

A former student, Aaron, showed up at the FCEC one day. He came by to let everyone know what changes had occurred in his life and claimed it was because of the people who took the time to teach him more than academic skills. He shared the importance of making him accountable for choices and responsible for his personal decisions that had made a difference in his life. Aaron entered our program due to his inability to follow rules and control his anger. He faced many obstacles including incarceration. After being out on his own for a few years, Aaron wanted to share that he was committed to helping other young men make better decisions before facing the consequences that he faced.

Aaron hooked up with a local youth ministry group and is training to work with young boys to support them in a positive manner. Aaron came back to the FCEC and spoke with the group of guys to encourage them to make good decisions. His experiences were well received because he had once been in their shoes. The students in the group were encouraged by his presentation as they could relate personal experiences to Aaron's journey.

A-SCHOOL BOOK PATROL

Designed to encourage reading for students, the focus of the A-School Book Patrol is reviewing books for elementary students. Students will provide the reviews on the school system website. This group will read books from the elementary school reading lists and provide feedback with ratings to encourage the elementary students to read. Review forms were designed to be user-friendly for the FCEC students to communicate via the web. A great tool that can be used by all elementary schools, it combines reading with technology while promoting books. The FCEC students will also be improving their own reading skills in the process.

BOYS 2 MEN

The objective of this MIA: Mission in Action group is to provide reading material to economically disadvantaged members of the community. Through researching the community, the students discovered that economically disadvantaged students' reading performance was lower than that of other groups. The students indicated this was due to the lack of reading materials available. Additionally, the students determined that many economically disadvantaged students do not have reading material at home. Books are seen as a luxury by such families and not crucial to meeting the survival needs in the household.

Students collected books donated from various community sources including individuals, schools, and agencies. The books were distributed to various target locations in the community such as the Boys and Girls Clubs, shelters, community centers, and agencies that work with economically disadvantaged people. Labels were placed in the books with a challenge to read the book and then pass it on to others. Hundreds of books were distributed.

Here is an example for the Boys 2 Men program developed by the students and facilitated by the teacher. It addresses the 10 service-learning components defined by Institute for Global Education and Service Learning.

BOYS 2 MEN:
READING TO ROME ACTION PLAN

I. Preparation/Planning

    A. Essential Question: How can students at the FCEC promote/increase reading literacy within the Rome/Floyd County Community through service learning?

    B. Goal: To provide books to the people of Rome/Floyd County.

    C. Issue: According to SchoolMatters (2007) student performance in Georgia in reading proficiency is 86.6 percent for the school year 2005. That is above the AYP target of 66.7 percent; however, the economically disadvantaged reading score (79.8 percent) and black students' score (80.6 percent) are lower than the white students (91.6 percent). The students indicated this is due to the lack of reading materials available within home settings. Additionally, the students determined that many economically disadvantaged students do not have reading material at home.

II. Meaningful Service

Books will be collected through various donations. They will be distributed to families at the Boys & Girls Club in Rome, the Rome/Floyd Parks and Recreation facilities, after school groups, Floyd County Health Department, Highland Rivers, Open Door Home, Homeless Shelter, Floyd County Court System, Battered Women's Shelter, and to various agencies/services that serve the target groups. The books will encompass all genres and benefit all ages.

III. Reflection

    A. Journal: Each student will write a reflection of each day's activities and participation.

    B. Group Discussion: Students meet to discuss ways to improve the collection/distribution of books. New ideas are also shared with input from each group member.

IV. Participant Voice

Students will meet to decide on issues addressed in this project and compare data from past projects. A group leader and transcriber will be selected by their peers. Students will research data on community poverty issues, along with state testing data. Discussion of issues will determine if the focus on reading involvement and lack of materials in the hands of the economically disadvantaged and black students are factors in test discrepancy. Students will record information and discuss ways to improve the reading discrepancy.

V. Genuine Need

After completing various research projects relating to the issue, the students will decide if the one factor to improve reading vocabulary and comprehension is to read more. Many students read because they are required to, but not many do because they want to!

VI. Connection to Learning

Curriculum Alignment:

NCLB: All students are to be grade proficient by the year 2014.
GPS: Georgia Performance Standards addressed are:

    1. The student participates in discussions related to curricular learning in all subject areas (ELA9RC2).

    2. The student establishes a context for information acquired by reading across subject areas (ELA9RC4).

    3. The student uses research and technology to support writing (ELA9W3).

    4. The student participates in student-to-teacher, student-to-student, and group verbal interactions (ELALSV1).

    5. The student formulates reasoned judgments about written and oral communication in various media genres. The student delivers focused, coherent, and polished presentations that convey a clear and

distinct perspective, demonstrate solid reasoning, and combine traditional rhetorical strategies of narration, exposition, persuasion, and description (ELA9LSV2).

6. The student will describe how thoughtful and effective participation in civic life is characterized by obeying the law, paying taxes, serving on a jury, participating in the political process, performing public service, registering for military duty, being informed about current issues, and respecting differing opinions (SSCG7).
7. Students will organize, interpret, and make inferences from statistical data (MM4D).
8. Students will solve problems (using appropriate technology) (MM1P1).
9. Students will make connections among mathematical ideas to other disciplines (MM1P4).
10. Students will identify and investigate problems scientifically (SCSh3).
11. Students will demonstrate the computation and estimation skills necessary for analyzing data and developing reasonable scientific explanations (SCSh5).

VII. Diversity

Recognizing and respecting different cultures and beliefs are critical to meeting the needs of the community through reading literacy. Distributing reading materials to families in need will be done at various community events. Venues are reflective of meeting a diversified need throughout the community.

VIII. Partnerships

Other groups involved with this project include:

- Floyd County Employees
- 100 Black Men of Rome
- NAACP Youth Group
- Individual Community Members

IX. Assessment

- Self-assessment at end of project
- Attendance/participation in community events
- Collection/distribution of material

X. Evaluation

- Written evaluation
- Availability of reading material for community
- Data of books collected/distributed to households
- Teacher evaluation
- Written documentation

PLAYHOUSE PROJECT

The Playhouse Project was a school-wide activity that involved all the students at the nontraditional school. This project was developed when one of the elementary schools in the system needed a playhouse for the students who were confined to wheelchairs. The school's parent/teacher organization provided the funding. The students selected various committees for each of the components that were decided upon at a meeting led by the school counselor.

The foreman of the construction committee made the contact with a local builder to help with the design and layout of the building, along with the codes required for construction. The builder met with the construction crew to explain the processes associated with creating a playhouse for student use. The builder would supervise the building, working side-by-side with students.

Another committee was responsible for controlling the finances and ordering materials at the best prices. The students created price lists and discussed options. The committee made phone calls and ordered the materials needed. Files were made to check invoices against delivered materials, along with additional expenses.

Other committees included a decorating committee responsible for making the playhouse inviting for the students to use, a transport committee that had to arrange for the building to be moved to the site, and a clean-up committee.

The Playhouse Project showed the relevance of all academic studies to real-life experiences. Social skills and work skills were developed throughout this activity. The project took several months to complete but was a tremendous success for the students.

CELEBRATIONS

At the close of each semester the students are honored with a luncheon to celebrate accomplishments. It is vital for students to celebrate and see the results of the efforts put into completing a project. Sponsored by local community groups, the luncheons are provided to also teach appropriate social skills when attending a formal event. Students are given etiquette lessons stressing table manners, appropriate conversation topics, and dress.

The lessons focus on topics such as first impressions, introductions, greetings and shaking hands, paying and receiving compliments, family dining table manners, and polite conversation at a dinner table. The students are able to invite a significant adult, not a parent, who has been a positive influence in their lives. Other guests are invited, including local and state probation officers, school administrators, system administrators, community volunteers, and members of the school board.

The students are the honored guests and are served by the staff. Various themes are used as the cafeteria is turned into a beautiful dining area. It has been amazing to see that many students have never eaten at a table for a meal with real dishes. Even through the celebration event, the students are learning skills essential for life after school.

Service-learning projects have been very successful for our students. Here are a few of the responses from the student reflection journals about various projects:

"I've learned to be happy with what I have and donate (items) once in a while. I learned to give people stuff."

"I learned teamwork, self-discipline, and tidiness. These are very important things to know later on into adulthood."

"This experience makes me feel better about myself. I feel I have helped someone else. I learned the world doesn't revolve around me. I've challenged myself. I am giving to the community."

"This activity helped me realize my full potential and how much volunteer work means to me and my community."

"It allows us to help others and to better ourselves. It also allows us to see how unfortunate others can be. By seeing this, it lets us see that we have no reason to complain."

"You should be nice to people. I will be different in the future."

"I love to help kids and see them smile."

"I have more understanding for the mental[ly] ill people—they don't always have help. If people would help them, it would be better off for them."

"I learned by helping others and working together we get more accomplished. We are leaders."

"I have learned that not everyone has as much as me. Some people need donations. I have a better understanding of why people donate stuff."

Service learning has proven to be a proactive move to help students see the relevance of academic learning and real life situations. The various projects are for the students "eye openers" to the needs of others. Making the connection has instilled a sense of belonging and caring that otherwise these students might not experience.

· 3 ·

A-B-C It's Easy as 1-2-3

Academic Strategies

It's not that you can make a difference; it's that everything you do makes a difference.

—Philippe Cousteau

𝒯oday's generations of students have witnessed firsthand horrific events that have trickled down into their daily lives. From school violence such as Columbine (1999), to the Virginia Tech incident (2007), to the 9/11 events in which American soil was violated by terrorists, students have been exposed to devastating acts. While negative societal and world events and individuals can have a dramatic impact upon young minds, today's educators have the power to alter the destiny of children.

Solid support initiatives and communication among fellow colleagues, parents, and community members are essential in the journey of life. Working together and visualizing a bright future for tomorrow's generation of students necessitates a commitment to taking risks, embracing the uniqueness of individuals, and ultimately empowering students to take ownership of their education. The solution lies in educators caring enough to encourage the students to find their passion and pursue their dreams.

Many other strategies are used in the nontraditional education center to empower students to take ownership of their learning. Providing opportunities for the students to embrace their educational journey enables them to see they belong in the driver's seat of their future. The students are discovering the need to belong in school and not to alienate themselves from the academic components. They become part of the team, not the object of decisions made for them. These ideas have been developed by teachers who work with at-risk students. The teachers see the successes that come from incorporating the strategies in their classrooms.

INTRAMURALS

The students enrolled in the nontraditional education program cannot participate in any extracurricular activity at their home school. While many of the students enjoy sports, music, art, and other outside activities, they do not have access to these privileges. Teenagers need to be able to get rid of the excess energy that has accumulated throughout the school day. Intramural tournaments are a great opportunity to reinforce self-discipline and team-building skills through structured activity.

The physical education teacher offers various intramural activities for the students after school. He or she offers times for teams to practice and prepare for the single-elimination tournaments. Students select the teams and create their own game plans with guidelines established by the teacher. For example, one of the guidelines may state that each team must have at least one middle school member. Another one may include something like only one player per team who has played on their school team may be on the field, or court, at one time. The guidelines are used to help balance the competition. It is exciting to see the teams create t-shirts and have fun with the other students to enjoy the competitiveness in the air.

Students who do not participate in the actual activity will stay after school to watch the competitions. It is a great opportunity for the staff of the nontraditional education center to have fun with the students and parents in a fun environment of friendly competition. The winning team gets bragging rights and also receives prizes from the school. Every student who participates in the intramural game receives recognition and prizes given out at an assembly.

WEIGHT TRAINING

Weight training is another opportunity for students to develop self-discipline and a better sense of well-being through better lifestyle choices. Students interested in staying after school to train with a coach are able to develop a weight training program that is self-paced and does not compete with other participants. A weight training chart (see appendix A) is designed for each participant and monitored by the instructor. Students are able to set weekly goals and chart progress.

One of the greatest successes of the weight training program is that students are developing life-long habits that encourage healthier living. Many of the students have never participated in weight training, for various reasons. The instructor works with each student individually to develop the best program determined by the goals set. Several students have continued to lift weights after completing the program.

IN-SCHOOL SUSPENSION

Students are assigned in-school suspension (ISS) when disruptive behavior or violation of school policies prevents the child from being successful during the school day. The purpose of the ISS program is to provide a setting, apart from the regular classroom, where a student may continue academic progress in an environment free from social interaction. ISS is a "time out" place where a student can regroup and get back on target for completion without suffering academic consequences.

The ISS program is very structured, with rules and guidelines that address student behaviors and provide class work assigned by the academic teachers for the students. Students assigned to ISS report directly to the classroom upon arrival to school. They are given the rules and assigned a seat for their entire stay.

Assignments may range from one block to nine days. The student remains with the paraprofessional for the assigned time. Academic assignments are sent by each student's teachers to be completed in the ISS classroom. The paraprofessional in ISS collects the completed assignments and returns the work to the teachers, who grade the completed assignments.

Students are also given additional assignments to complete that address the behavior(s) that caused the assignment and focus on making better decisions in the future. Each student creates a self-improvement behavior plan of action while serving in the ISS program. This plan of action focuses on behavior improvement with options available to curtail future disruptions. Magazine articles relating to the offense are also provided to help each student prevent future discipline offenses. Depending on the amount of time assigned to ISS, the student will complete one to three essays. Topics for the essays relate to goal setting and include:

1. What Do You Really Want?
2. Important People to You
3. What Inspires You?

The ISS program is a good deterrent to suspending students out of school. It provides an opportunity for students to regroup, refocus, and rededicate themselves to reaching individual goals for improvement. Keeping students in school is a must, and ISS is a great accountability tool if used effectively.

SUPER SATURDAY

One year 12 seniors were enrolled who were scheduled to graduate on time. This was the largest group of seniors ever enrolled at the nontraditional school at one time. It posed a huge challenge for the staff as many of the seniors hit the midpoint of their last semester and decided they would try to coast through the last few weeks of high school. Several of the seniors were not failing; however, they were headed in that direction. No matter what was said to encourage these students the pattern of poor performance continued.

Anyone who has dealt with students in this situation knows the difficulty of motivating seniors to stay focused in the last few weeks before graduation. Parents were frustrated, and so was the staff, with the passive attitudes presented by the seniors. After repeated parent conferences and phone calls it was decided to face the situation with what the students valued—their weekend time.

Students who waste time during academic courses often get a special treat by attending Super Saturday. Super Saturday is designed for students unwilling to complete assignments during class time. Super Saturday begins at 8:00 a.m. sharp and ends around 11:00 a.m. The purpose is to show the importance of managing time. If a student chooses to waste academic time, then the student gives up free time that is afforded him or her on Saturday morning. It does not take long for students to realize that wasting school time is not nearly as critical as giving up their free weekend time. Teachers give the missing assignments to the administrator, and students complete these assignments during Super Saturday.

Super Saturday is for any student who has a chance to pass his or her academic classes. Students attend if their grades are borderline due to not completing homework or class work assignments; due to failing a test and being given the opportunity to retake it; or for having excessive absences and needing to make up missed time. It is also a time where students who need to complete community service may work around the school.

The work assigned has already been taught in the classroom; therefore, students only need to complete it. No new material is used during Super Saturday. Students may also come into the computer lab and practice for the end-of-course tests (EOCTs), Criterion-Reference Competency Test (CRCT), and Georgia High School Graduation Test (GHSGT) using various prep programs offered by the school system.

Super Saturday is not held every Saturday. It is scheduled on an as-needed basis. Usually around the midterm, or close to the end of a grading period, is a good indication of falling grades. Teachers may notice a decline in the efforts of the students on their class work and homework of the students. Students are given ample time to complete assignments.

Students and parents are informed in advance of Super Saturday. A written letter is sent home, and parents must sign off for their child to attend. It is not required, but strongly encouraged, for students to take advantage of this opportunity. It is also a good source of documentation of parent involvement. What a great discovery! The change was almost immediate in the performance levels of the seniors from the Super Saturday experience. All 12 seniors graduated on time.

GUARDIAN ANGELS

This strategy was put into place when many of the students were coming to school without ample supplies or encouragement. It appeared that many students were arriving to school without adult guidance and supervision. The precept behind Guardian Angels is to provide the extra care of making sure the students were in the right mindset to face the school day. Many of the students are from dysfunctional home environments that are not like many of the homes of traditional students. These students need caring adults to have the same opportunity that so many others take for granted.

Staff members divide the students up evenly to make sure the students have everything needed for the day. The students are not aware of the assignment. The staff members greet their children and check to make sure the students have homework and supplies and have eaten a good breakfast. Each staff member keeps progress checks with teachers to create a supportive working atmosphere for the student at school. Many students will share problems that are going on outside of school with the staff member and often are relieved to have someone who listens and actually cares.

This strategy is a win-win situation for all involved. The students feel a stronger connection toward school because of the extra support. The teacher is doing what is necessary to clear the path of education from outside distractions. The strategy gives a chance for the students to focus and concentrate on academics rather than worry about survival. The staff will share concerns of the students during the afternoon staff meeting and try to come up with solutions to help the students where feasible.

Kari was one such student who found solace and comfort from one of the teachers. Kari's home situation was deplorable. Often the utilities were shut off because mom would fail to pay the bills. Mom had problems with addiction to prescription medication and would neglect to take care of the responsibilities of parenting Kari. Issues of providing appropriate clothing, food, and doctor appointments would go unattended at home. Older siblings and their children also crammed into the tiny living area, causing chaos much of the time. Needless to say, Kari's academic journey was the least of her concerns. She was a middle school student headed straight to the dropout line.

One of the teachers chose to serve Kari as her Guardian Angel. This teacher immediately recognized the neglect issues with Kari after a brief conversation. The teacher began finding the good areas in Kari and working with her on her self-confidence. Kari was an excellent writer, so she began writing her struggles in a journal each day. The teacher would guide Kari to take charge over the situations that Kari could control. The main area was her education.

Kari began to improve her grades. She would make a good grade and immediately show the teacher. The teacher would often find clothes and other surprises for Kari. If Kari had a good week, the teacher would have a special lunch or something else to show the appreciation was there. Kari needed extra support, and it was provided by a teacher.

As the months progressed, Kari improved and brought her grades to passing with high marks. Kari was at school every time the doors were opened because she knew the guidance and support were provided. The teacher also kept in close contact with the mother. The mother would occasionally clean up her act; however, she was inconsistent.

The Guardian Angel program has been an important addition by reaching out and giving the students an opportunity to belong.

PROJECT-BASED LEARNING

Each year it is a goal to improve the service-learning program by incorporating ideas shared in the student survey results and observations of the stakeholders. Beginning this past year, service learning was expanded to project-based, standards-focused learning. The Buck Institute for Education created a handbook called *Project Based Learning* (Markham 2003) that was instrumental in helping the staff to go one step further in clarifying the relationship of academics to real-life, student-directed learning. Standards-focused, project-based learning allowed us to not only utilize successful components of service learning but allowed for incorporating the Georgia Performance Standards.

Project-based learning is a systematic teaching method engaging students in learning knowledge and skills through an extended inquiry process structured around complex, authentic questions and carefully designed products and tasks with various methods of assessment. Students are guided through the curriculum by a driving (essential) question or authentic problem creating a need for the students to know the material, not just read and answer questions. It is designed for teachers to create a high-performing classroom where the group forms a powerful learning community focused on achievement, self-mastery, and contribution to the community.

Where service-learning projects are done outside the academic classrooms as extra activities using the academic knowledge, project-based learning takes service learning inside the academic classrooms. The projects are the driving factor in the curriculum, giving students ownership and a voice in the development of the activity based on standards. Students are actively engaged in the design and outcome of each project using a more in-depth approach that involves critical thinking, problem solving, and dissemination of information.

Collaboration and teamwork are essential components to discovering relevance while developing relationships by working together. The culminating project is the end result of meeting the standards. This approach offers a variety of assessment tools, and the final evaluation is based on more than a simple paper-and-pencil exam. Research shows that knowledge, thinking, doing, and the contexts for learning are all tied together. Project-based learning is designed to create new instructional practices that reflect the environment where students live and learn, showing relevance to academic learning.

Two examples of project-based learning are given. "An Ounce of Prevention" (see appendix B) is based on a book read by high school English/language arts students that focuses on teen issues. Today's teens deal with many issues that often lead to teen depression. Students need to realize and reflect on how their actions and words can lead to teen depression and, in some cases, suicide.

Another example, from a high school physical education class, is called "How Is Obesity More Than Just Being Overweight?" (see appendix C), in which students identify and investigate some of the areas that contribute to obesity and how our society classifies or views obese people.

GOAL SHEET

Goal sheets are provided in each class and designed to empower students to map out their assignments for each day (see appendix D). Giving the students the opportunity to choose how they will complete the activities gives the students freedom and responsibility. There may be two or three activities listed for the class, and the student will prioritize the order in which they are completed. This enables students to have ownership into the class without the teacher relinquishing instruction. The end results are the same. The goal sheets are placed in the students' portfolios to be used in the assessment of meeting requirements of each class.

CHANCE TO ADVANCE

This program was designed to enable middle school students who have failed at least one grade level and are behind their peers to receive extra help in academic skills. Many of the students have performed poorly in academic studies and are at high risk for dropping out of school. Whether the students have been retained due to poor grades, attendance, or other reasons, they have also increased their chances of becoming a dropout.

The students who participate in the Chance to Advance program receive basic skills training in the academic content areas. The students are assigned to one educator who serves as the advisor, or liaison, for the term. Each learner is issued a notebook that contains guidelines of the course work that is in addition to the regular assignments needed to pass the grade level and master skills.

The notebook contains checks and balances that serve as accountability and reward the success of the program. This allows students to see immediate rewards and consequences associated with school-based decisions. Additionally, the learners gain a sense of the importance of positive behavior associated with successful academic performance. Students learn life skills and are issued bank checks and registers for the assigned activities.

The group of students reports to the advisor each morning for a meeting. It usually lasts between 15 to 30 minutes to discuss the outlook for the day and check the skills lesson of the previous day. Equipped with necessary supplies, the students attend each regular class throughout the school day and report back to the advisor at the close of the day. The advisor works on basic skills with each student each afternoon as an extra class period. Each student works on the weaknesses exhibited in each academic area.

This strategy can be implemented with anyone working with youth. It would be easily adaptable in any after-school program that helps students by creating coupons and rewards that enable youth to see immediate rewards for work well done. This would also be beneficial with religious groups or clubs designed to work with youth. Parents can also design a program to help students learn responsibilities at home or in their community.

PORTFOLIO ASSESSMENT

What happens to all the work a student accumulates throughout the term? Will you find it stuffed in a locker? Crammed into a book bag? Under the bed with who knows what else? What does a student have to show for the hard work of a term other than a grade on the report card? Each student at the nontraditional school keeps his or her work in a notebook or folder and creates a portfolio when the assignments are completed.

The portfolio consists of assignments that show the student's progress throughout the term. Each teacher provides a list of assignments, and the students are responsible for organizing it and making it presentable to be returned to their home school. The portfolio is designed to "show off" the students' progress. Many students have no idea how much they have accomplished until they collect their term's work and create a presentable product. The portfolio represents accomplishments of any activity that is completed at the school.

Other pieces of information are also placed in the portfolio. Included in the portfolio are instructions for leading a conference from the student's point of view, a work evaluation form for each academic area, a "How I See Myself" self-evaluation form, assessments, service-learning time sheets, tier-level sheets, progress or report cards, and a conference agenda. If students participate in any other activity at school, evidence such as certificates or evaluations are included.

Pre- and post-assessment information is included to show reading and math levels upon entering and upon exiting the program. Students who attend the anger management classes have a record of the class in their portfolio. Service-learning project information is included. Anything to promote student learning is included.

The portfolio is also used in student-led conferences. The student is responsible for collecting the materials and being prepared to discuss the contents with adults attending the conference. Parents or guardians are able to see firsthand what the learner has, or has not, mastered or accomplished while at the school. If the student is doing poorly in a class, then he or she can provide evidence of what areas need to be strengthened. If the learner refuses to complete an assignment, the teachers provide documentation to show evidence of reasoning why the student failed to complete the assignment. This documentation is given when a student does not turn in an assignment; the teacher provides a sheet that the student completes with an explanation written by the student about the assignment.

Overall, the portfolio serves as a scrapbook of the student's time spent in the nontraditional educational environment. The student will hopefully look at opportunities that were provided and see his or her individual successes in accomplishing tasks. Many students are amazed at the accomplishments they achieved when they look at the portfolio.

STUDENT-LED CONFERENCES

Student-led conferences provide students with an opportunity to talk with significant adults about their educational progress. Each student invites his or her parents or guardians and teachers to attend a meeting concerning the student's educational goals and progress in meeting those goals. The meetings are facilitated by the student and follow an agenda that the student has developed prior to the conference with the assistant principal.

During the meeting, the student shares his or her educational goals and examples of his or her portfolio. The student analyzes his or her strengths and weaknesses and reflects upon the educational consequences of choices the student has made. Together, the student, teachers, and parents determine what each will do to assist the student to move closer to reaching the educational goals. Forms, handouts, and suggestions are provided to enable students, parents, and teachers to reap maximum benefits from each conference. Any stakeholder involved with the students can request a conference.

Students are also responsible for conducting student-led conferences during the semester. The parents, students, and teachers receive training about the student-led conferences using the guide "Student-Led Conferences" from Conway Middle School, located in Louisville, Kentucky. Student-led conferences have many benefits to all stakeholders involved, which include, but are not limited to, the following.

Student Benefits

1. Gaining accountability for their learning
2. Gaining greater commitment to school work and learning
3. Building self-confidence and self-esteem
4. Encouraging student-parent communication
5. Building communication and critical-thinking skills
6. Placing responsibility on the student and parent
7. Allowing students to take ownership and become actively involved

Parent Benefits

1. Increasing the amount of information given to the parents
2. Learning more about their child's learning and skills

3. Gaining an opportunity to help their student set positive goals
4. Becoming active participants in their child's learning
5. Providing same-language communication
6. Eliminating standing in line waiting for a conference

Teacher Benefits

1. Placing less stress on teachers; very relaxed atmosphere
2. Allowing less confrontational (more positive) interaction
3. Placing responsibility on student and parent
4. Increasing parent participation

Perhaps the greatest benefit for all is that this type of conferencing takes away the blame game. No one is pointing fingers or being accused of picking on a student. Everyone works collectively for a resolution. Parents, students, and school officials all take part in a discussion to seek the best way to help the student become successful.

READING AND WRITING WORKSHOPS

The high school English/language arts teacher has designed workshops for the students. These workshops are special days set aside from the routine and designed to encourage reading and writing outside the normalcy of strictly essay construction or guided reading.

Students look forward to these workshops as they help establish the parameters used in writing. The room is set up for refreshments and a relaxed environment, much like a coffee shop. During the writing workshop the emphasis is placed on creative writing. Students create character profiles, mood, and setting and explore all options to real-life choices, supporting opinions through writing.

Persuasive writing is learning to take a stand on an issue and then supporting it with writing. It may be done through poetry, music lyrics, or other forms. Students are responsible for having a writer's notebook and materials for this session. Students learn to self-edit to finish a final product and publish the results in a legible and correct manner.

The reading workshop requires novels read by the students to be on the approved reading list for the genre of the class. Students have standards requiring a number of novels to be read each semester. This workshop is a time where students can relax and read freely. The only requirement is that each student keeps a reading log of information read for the block. The reading log serves as a summary of the book and is useful when it is time to complete projects based on the novel.

JOURNAL WRITING

The high school English/language arts teacher and the middle school English/language arts teacher both incorporate a journal-writing activity daily in their classes. The students write a journal entry as a warm-up activity at the beginning of class. The teachers do not personally read the entries as students are encouraged to write freely about feelings and events of the day. The students are told not to incriminate themselves by discussing anything illegal in the journal that could cause any legal ramifications. Students are graded on length and participation, not on spelling and grammar.

This activity's purpose is for students to get into the habit of writing. Many students use it as a sounding board or to let out frustrations, while others use it as an ongoing story. It is amazing that many of the students want the teachers to read the journals. It is effective in getting the mindset for the lesson and putting away distractions that might interrupt learning.

INDIVIDUALIZED PHYSICAL EDUCATION

Roger Dewey, a retired teacher, developed a system to incorporate a variety of physical education classes that focused on individual performance per class requirements. Dewey worked a majority of his career in a traditional school prior to wrapping up his career in a nontraditional setting. Due to the size of the nontraditional education center, physical education classes were grouped together where in one given block of time many students may be taking three or four different class sessions. The students have not reached success in a traditional school; therefore, following established procedures and ways of instruction would be foolish and unproductive.

The basis of the program was to allow as much student decision making as possible and still have a worthwhile program of fitness and physical education. The empowerment is centered on the planning sheets the students complete daily prior to starting their selected activity (see appendix E) and a sample of a completed activity sheet (see appendix F).

The planning sheets give the students a chance to plan out their program for the day and include documentation of the warm-up activity, physical activities selected for the day, and a reflection at the end of the block to show progress in reaching the individual's predetermined goal for the week. This enables students to focus on individual progress and not be competitive with others in the class. Even in team sport situations, each student focuses on individual progress.

During the reflection students provide feedback to the instructor on areas in which the activities could be improved to maximize the purpose. Students are encouraged to suggest better activities, class procedures, and other items that would improve the program. Individual conferences are also held by the instructor to get input for program improvements.

Restrictions are placed on the students in planning for each class. Equipment, space, and safety are the major areas of concern since these are limited. The available equipment is used in a manner that allows all students the opportunity to participate during the given class time.

Students are also empowered by evaluating the program each semester. This evaluation is written as a reflection for optimal communication of the program and is graded as part of the final exam for the class. Opinions of the students are not graded, but ideas for improvement are used to increase performance of the program.

PASS TUTORING

Dr. Amy Allee designed this program several years ago to enhance academic learning. The Providing Assistance, Supporting Students (PASS) tutoring is a 45-minute session four days a week for students who need extra help. Each academic area teacher takes one day per week to provide extra assistance to students who are struggling in the given area. For example, Monday is science, Tuesday is math, Wednesday is social studies, and Thursday is English/language arts. The high school instructor helps the students individually and collectively during this after-school session. Students are often allowed to make up low scores on tests, quizzes, class work, and even homework assignments.

Several teachers use this time to review for tests or help students complete projects. Students who are taking mandated state tests also take advantage of this program. The assistant principal provides support by working on test preparations online to assist the students. PASS is just an added support to help the students who may need the extra push or lack the support in the home. Parents are sometime overwhelmed with the constant changes in the curriculum and the demands of work.

PRINCIPAL POW WOW

The principal pow wow is designed to motivate the unmotivated students who are refusing to complete assignments. This group is led by the principal or a designee. Students report to this session for a special period after or before school to complete missed assignments not completed in the classroom. Students may have been absent and not completed any make-up work or may have simply refused to work in class.

The length of the session is 30 minutes each day, and the students report until missed work is made up to the teacher's satisfaction. It is a great way for the principal to help the students refocus on academics and build relationships by providing extra support to the teachers and parents.

CHESS TOURNAMENT

Designed to promote critical thinking, self-discipline, and social development skills, this activity was introduced in the special education department. Students were taught the rules and regulations of the game and began playing as a reward for completion of assignments. The teacher took the opportunity to incorporate the social studies curriculum into the game through the history and origin of chess. This piqued the interest of the students, and they began to study the various countries associated with the history.

The educator brought in chess games with different themes, and the students studied the history of each set. The students began playing chess at every free opportunity—before and after school and during their lunch. Their involvement sparked the curiosity of other students; therefore, the teacher had his students teaching other students how to play. At the end of the term the special education teacher and his students organized a tournament for any student in the school. It was exciting and created a fun and creative competition with learning as a bonus.

These strategies are used in the classrooms at the nontraditional education center; however, any program working with at-risk students can adapt these ideas to meet the needs of the learners. The value of sharing them is to take what will work, disregard what will not work, and adapt the ideas to promote individuals within their own environment. Civic organizations can create teams to develop projects to improve the cause of their program. Church leaders can use these to help create partnerships and involvement with youth. Neighborhood groups can get together to create solutions using these strategies.

As anyone can see, it takes a sense of caring and building relationships with at-risk youth. Teens today have a great sense of leadership and talents that promote strong ethics and character. Take time to listen to what they say without judging them by standards defined by the older generation.

Academic strategies used in a nontraditional education program are the focus of this chapter. Several strategies are detailed with an emphasis on building relationships with students. Personal stories are provided to show the importance of providing assistance to the at-risk learners. School-wide strategies as well as individual classroom strategies offer methods to provide ownership to at-risk learners and connect them to academic learning.

· 4 ·

From Zeroes to Heroes

The Tier Factor Program Behavior Strategy

We must become the change we want to see.

—Gandhi

*H*ave you ever accidently turned down a one-way street to find yourself stuck going in a direction you did not want to go? Perhaps you became confused, lost, and ultimately panicked by the rapid pace of darting automobiles with no exit signs in sight. It's happened to everyone at one time during his or her life. What a relief it must have been when you saw a sign that led you in the right direction. Perhaps pulling over to ask someone directions was the key to getting back on the right road! Being a teenager is a lot like being a panicked driver: everything seems so out of control and overwhelming.

Everyone needs direction in his or her life from time to time, and being a teenager is no exception. Discipline or structure can be that direction! Discipline does not compromise direction; it is direction when planned and executed in an appropriate manner. While teenagers may adamantly claim they do not need discipline because they are "grown," in actuality the need for order and structure associated with discipline is craved. Discipline is not simply a way to invoke punishment; in truth it is a caring individual taking the time to provide positive direction and guidance.

Acknowledging and addressing difficult issues and ultimately developing a means of preventing undesired behaviors from reoccurring is critical in both parenting and educating a child. The truth is that there are no GPS devices available when it comes to parenting or educating a child. What a joy it would be if we could just type in a destination for our children, one in which the child never experiences the harshness of the world. Unfortunately, the world does not operate this way. Children may experience detours or bumps in the road that veer off the intended course.

49

If discipline is a one-way street with no place for turning around, what role does an educator serve in safely directing a child to stay on the right path? While the journey toward becoming responsible citizens is easier for some than others, the lives of many American children have been and continue to be marred by circumstances both in and out of their control. The difficulties and lack of support many children receive at home often find their way to the schoolhouse door.

Have you ever witnessed a small child carrying a backpack loaded down with books, the child's shoulders slumped, back arched, head hung from the strain of the books? This is the way millions of children come to school in America each day. Except it is not just the backpacks that are weighing the children down; it is the strain of family issues such as financial situations, custody issues, and interpersonal relationships that are burdening the lives of children. The reality is that certain children act out, join gangs, and commit violent acts because they are desperate for two things: love and discipline.

Students want discipline, order, and structure with established limits and boundaries created for them to succeed in society. The major conflict students have with discipline in school is that the discipline has no meaning or connection to them. School discipline needs to be meaningful and clearly defined. Discipline is not writing lines for not completing homework or being off task in a class. Discipline is not being assigned detention or suspension for not following rules. Consequences and discipline are totally different.

Discipline includes guidelines for classroom procedures given for all to follow. A clear set of expectations for success is vital. Discipline involves a process of establishing rules that provide an orderly and safe environment with an encouraging learning atmosphere where each individual has the opportunity to be productive. Discipline is not about control. It is guidance toward shaping a child to make wise choices, listen to his or her conscience, and live a life of meaning.

Many people misuse the word *discipline*. Schools establish discipline policies to address misbehavior and rule violations. Not addressed is the understanding of what is positive and fallible in directing students to perform appropriately. According to *Encarta World English Dictionary*, *discipline* is defined as "training to ensure proper behavior; the practice or methods of teaching and enforcing acceptable patterns of behavior; order and control; a controlled orderly state, especially in a class of schoolchildren; calm controlled behavior; the ability to behave in a controlled and calm way even in a difficult or stressful situation."

What the faculty at FCEC has discovered in the nontraditional education environment is that students want immediate feedback when it relates to behavior. Years of experience, dedication, and commitment to assisting at-risk students has led to the development of a system to monitor behavior called the Tier Factor. It is similar to a point system that is used in regular education; however, it is also very different. It is designed as a proactive tool for students to recognize the appropriate behavior in each classroom while receiving immediate feedback on individual performance.

Expectations placed on educators and students vary. Students will respond to how high the bar is set. It is disappointing for a student to be in class following the expectations and guidelines that have been defined by the educator only to be punished because a majority of the students have chosen to not follow the rules. Some educators become very frustrated and lash out with a class consequence. What is this saying to the student who is meeting the expectations and then is serving a punishment because of the teacher's frustration? Students may believe they are being great and following expectations when they are misguided because of teacher frustration.

Times change; children change. The faculty members are cognizant of change and the need to respond. There was a need to revamp the point system that had been in place since the founding of the nontraditional education program. The point system used in previous years was based solely on behavior performance. The point system was no longer effective and warranted an upgrade. It had become a deterrent rather than a positive performance indicator due to the students' lack of empathy toward behavior issues. Students who were making poor decisions in their behavior were still making great strides in academic performance and attendance. Due to losing points for behavior, students still had to suffer the consequences regardless of the other areas of improvement. The teachers used the system differently in their classes and were the sole identifiers of the behavior violations.

Bonnie Benard (1991) identified critical protective factors that were found to provide resilience that strengthens an individual's ability to survive and thrive in education. The protective factors include caring relationships, high expectation messages and positive beliefs, and opportunities to participate and contribute. These three protective factors are crucial to keeping students enthusiastically engaged and involved in school.

The first step toward determining what type of initiative would best serve learners was the gathering of information from the current students. A questionnaire was constructed in order to gain insight into the students' perceptions about the current point system and academic or behavioral issues. The student questionnaire was comprised of five questions that included:

1. What have been the strengths of attending the alternative school?
2. What would make this program better for students?
3. What is the role of the teachers at the alternative school?
4. What has helped you the most while attending the alternative school?

5. Explain how the alternative school program has/has not helped you become a better person.

The students were encouraged to freely express their concerns and ideas in order to promote ownership and gain valuable insight. Providing students with a voice and the freedom to express what works best for them is a key to developing an effective nontraditional school program. Often students are able to identify strengths or weaknesses that might have gone unnoticed, or deemed insignificant, by the faculty and staff.

The faculty members administering the questionnaire collected useful information because of the trustworthiness and ideas of students. Many of the students were surprised their opinions and ideas were valued by the staff. When the questionnaire was first offered, many of the students were hesitant to express their opinions. An amazing reaction occurred after the teachers explained the reason for the questionnaire and soothed anxieties, and a bounty of feedback poured in.

The students were inspired and excited to offer ideas for creating a new performance initiative within the school. By actively engaging students, it became evident that it takes all of the stakeholders in a school to make adjustments and improvements. Identification of improvement areas was possible without personal attacks and finger pointing based on personal beliefs.

After much introspection and examination of prior practices a new student performance initiative known as Tier Factor was created. Based on "experiential education," or learning by doing, the teachers, with student input, developed the Tier Factor program. It actively engages students in making appropriate decisions that directly impact progress. In an effort to empower students, promote increased student attendance, and improve academics and behaviors, the Tier Factor program relies on the student to complete personal ratings related to performance issues in these areas.

Based upon the belief that academics, behavior, and regular attendance are directly related, the creators of the Tier Factor program incorporated these three elements into a performance-based program in which students are directly responsible for their actions. Students are able to advance to higher tiers based upon academic performance, adherence to behavioral policies, and self-responsibility in attendance and social growth. In the same vein, students who do not meet certain requirements have consequences and are relegated to lower tiers. Incentives are incorporated into certain tiers in recognition of the students' progress and weekly achievements. The students are involved in selecting incentives that are meaningful and important to them.

While point systems based upon classroom behaviors are widely utilized within nontraditional schools, the creators of the Tier Factor program actively sought to engage students in developing realistic goals. Students are able to achieve academic and behavioral success through continual evaluation of practices, goal setting, ownership, and personal accountability.

Excuses are not acceptable, and students are not allowed to blame others for their lack of personal responsibility and success. The Tier Factor program teaches students to be accountable for actions and their consequences and to embrace ownership of their educational journey. Students are able to experience firsthand the rewards of succeeding in school. The Tier Factor program is an effective, positive means to have students be responsible for a brighter, more hopeful future. The Tier Factor program is designed to place students in the driver's seat and allow them to be the captain of the team!

Academics, behavior, and attendance (ABA) are the three essential components of the Tier Factor program. As noted earlier, grades, attendance, and behavior are early indicators of student success or failure and the risk of dropping out of school.

The Tier Factor program fosters student performance in the ABA areas. Students are responsible for creating and maintaining a portfolio in each academic area. Each day students record their daily classroom assignments and due dates on a student performance sheet. These sheets assist in keeping the students organized and aware of when assignments are due. At the end of each week, students reflect upon their individual classroom performances.

How does the Tier Factor system work? There are six general areas students are expected to follow in order for them to continue their educational journey:

1. Use appropriate language and dress
2. Be prepared for class (materials and assignments)
3. Use good manners and social behavior
4. Be on time for school and class
5. Be present at school (legal or medical note does not disrupt consecutive days)
6. Follow directions and guidelines of FCEC

Each teacher identifies specific classroom procedures and discusses in detail guidelines for success. Parents are also notified and given the opportunity to share comments and concerns with the teachers, signing a form acknowledging the process. Overall, the staff has developed a plan for immediate feedback with the students.

Every two weeks students are issued cards to be placed in lanyards with spaces for each block. Students are responsible for turning the cards in at the beginning of each class, and each teacher has a special stamp to use on the card. The stamp is given at the end of the class period.

The students are expected to follow the classroom procedures to earn a stamp for the class block. By successfully following the teacher's policies and procedures the student will earn a stamp for the class.

The student has the opportunity to earn one stamp for each of the four blocks. Failure to follow the teacher's policies and procedures will result in students not earning a stamp for that specific block.

At the end of the last block, the teacher will tally up the number of stamps each child has earned for that specific day. Students who have earned enough stamps will then be given a hole punch by the last block teacher. The hole punches are different for each teacher. The student will earn a hole punch if he or she has one of the following:

- Four blocks, four stamps
- Four blocks, three stamps

The student will not receive a hole punch if he or she has only one of the following:

- Four blocks, two stamps
- Four blocks, one stamp
- Four blocks, no stamps

Here is an example of a Tier Factor card, which can be white, blue, bronze, platinum, or platinum plus. It is a simple design that is easily made.

Figure 4.1.   Tier Factor Card

Tier level colors are as follows:

- *White card:* Upon enrollment each student receives a white card to begin the climb up the tier levels. A student begins to earn stamps and punches and is eligible to move up to the next level after three days. The student has no privileges or consequences on the white level.

NAME _____ Week: _____

Block	M	T	W	Th	F
1					
2					
3					
4					
Daily					

Figure 4.2.   White Card

- *Bronze card:* Assigned seating for students in the cafeteria during lunch and break. No classroom privileges or consequences. If student earns stamps and punches for six consecutive days he or she becomes eligible to move to the next level.

If a student MISSES even one stamp (but earns a hole punch) they will continue being bronze and the 6 Consecutive Day count will start over.

Block	M	T	W	TH	F
1					
2					
3					
4					
Daily					

Figure 4.3.   Bronze Card

- *Platinum card:* Being on a platinum card means the student has followed Tier Factor requirements and classroom guidelines and successfully completed all assignments as directed by all classroom teachers. The platinum card holder has the following privileges:

1. Early release to lunch and break (5 minutes)
2. May wear shorts that follow district policy

3. Preferential seating in cafeteria during lunch and break
4. May drink bottled water in class

When the student acquires nine consecutive days of stamps in all classes, he or she is eligible to move to the highest tier level.

Students earn Platinum after 6 consecutive days where they earn all stamps and hole punches.

Block	M	T	W	TH	F
1	●	●	●	●	●
2	●	●	●	●	●
3	●	●	●	●	●
4	●	●	●	●	●
Daily	✖	✖	✖	✖	✖

Figure 4.4.   Platinum Card

- *Platinum plus card:* This is the highest level on the Tier Factor rating. A student has exhibited excellence in meeting the requirements for other levels. The student has an A/B average in all classes and has earned the following privileges:

1. Early release to lunch and break (5 minutes) and first in lunch line
2. May wear shorts that follow district policy
3. May drink bottled water in class and eat a healthy snack
4. Preferential seating in cafeteria during lunch and break
5. Run errands for a teacher or help in office
6. Work in learning lab or participate in Wii Fitness/Sports for 20 minutes at discretion of teacher
7. Name placed in a drawing for a Principal's Choice reward. The rewards range from phone cards to iTune cards, movie passes, and whatever motivates the students.

Students earn Platinum Plus after 3 consecutive days of Platinum where they earn all stamps and hole punches.

Block	M	T	W	TH	F
1	●	●	●	●	●
2	●	●	●	●	●
3	●	●	●	●	●
4	●	●	●	●	●
Daily	✖	✖	✖	✖	✖

Figure 4.5.   Platinum Plus Card

- *Blue card:* The blue card is issued to students who have not been successful in the classroom. Students are assigned blue cards when they:

  1. fail to receive the appropriate stamps and punches to progress
  2. serve all-day detention, in-school suspension, or out-of-school suspension

- Students who earn a blue card are assigned silent lunch and break for three days in a designated area isolated from other students. The students stay on the blue card until they earn stamps and punches to move to another tier level.

Students earn Blue Level when they do not earn stamps or hole punches.

Block	M	T	W	TH	F
1	⬭	⬭			
2		⬭		⬭	
3		⬭		⬭	⬭
4	⬭	⬭		⬭	⬭
Daily		✖		✖	

Figure 4.6. Blue Card

Students wear the lanyards during the entire school day and return them to their fourth-block teachers at the end of the class. Lanyards are not to be taken home and must remain in the teacher's possession. Inside the clear area of a lanyard is a place to display the tier level card that corresponds to the student cards that a teacher will stamp and hole punch.

Additionally, any desecration of the lanyards or cards is a disciplinary matter. The lanyards and all associated material are property of the school. Students who commit fraud by attempting to swap or alter cards are automatically placed on blue level and subject to further disciplinary actions. All parties involved in the attempt to swap cards are treated in the same manner regardless of involvement. This is a serious matter that constitutes violation of the school's disciplinary policies.

Prior to the student moving from one tier level to another, a note signed by the teacher, parent, and student must be completed and turned in when the student arrives at school. This note is a great communication tool for all the stakeholders involved in the program. Absences are also part of the tier level process. If a student is absent from school a note must accompany the student upon returning.

The school district's attendance policy is very exact on what constitutes an excused or unexcused absence from school. A student's tier standing is not affected if he or she brings in a legal excuse; however, if a student is unexcused the tier level returns to a white card. The student must begin the process again to earn stamps and punches to progress. This has eliminated many unnecessary absences since the inception of this program.

What is so amazing about the Tier Factor program is the simplicity of it all. The students get so excited about receiving the stamps and hole punches. The Tier Factor program is a great tool for student documentation and can be easily adapted to fit any program that serves the youth. The teachers collect the tier level student cards and keep them as part of the student's portfolio. Although it seems childish and more in the line of kindergarten smiley faces, it really works.

Taylor had not met graduation requirements at his home school the previous year. He was charged with a felony not related to school and assigned to us for the remainder of the school year. Being a fifth-year senior was difficult for Taylor. He was belligerent, defiant, and mad at the world when he entered our school. He was determined to make life miserable for everyone around him, including his family, peers, and school staff.

Taylor constantly reminded everyone he was an adult (age 19) and that he did not belong in the alternative school. He treated others with an attitude that made others not like him. He would get mad at the principal and threatened to quit school. He did not care what he said or did to other people. Sadly, Taylor was really a caring person with deep emotional trust issues.

The teachers complained that he was disruptive in class and was not attempting his assignments. The students complained that he was being a pain in the rear by making inappropriate comments or laughing at them. His mother and stepfather would meet with the principal several times and would cooperate to the fullest extent. Many different tactics were tried to get Taylor to understand his responsibility for his education.

His mother and stepfather used their influence to get him to do his work at home. They stayed on top of the situation and kept in constant contact with the teachers and principal to help redirect Taylor. It was a constant battle. They popped in to check on Taylor and helped in every way possible. It would be wonderful if all parents would take the steps they did.

After meeting with the teachers, the principal moved Taylor out of some of his classes and had him work by himself. Taylor and the principal discussed his options and worked out a deal that allowed him to work by himself in a room across from the office. He could work in the room if he completed his assignments. He could also listen to his CDs as long as the noise did not leave the room and as long as the music was not a hindrance to his work. And he was free to gripe and complain, but only to the principal. He would do his work but not always his best. He stayed on the pass/fail borderline in two of his classes. Taylor needed additional time to complete his work. He had a difficult time concentrating and focusing on tasks.

Although the students at the nontraditional school were restricted from attending extracurricular activities, Taylor's situation was different because his felony charges were dismissed. He was allowed to attend his base school's extracurricular activities such as athletic events, prom, and senior activities.

He was still on the borderline of passing when the last progress reports were issued at the last six weeks of school. His mother, stepfather, and school officials communicated daily through phone calls, visits, and emails. Taylor's options were discussed, and it was decided Taylor would stay after school each day to complete assignments that were not finished. So Taylor stayed after school and often came in early to take tests, complete assignments, and do the necessary work.

The principal decided to try to make Taylor's last few weeks of school as enjoyable as possible, yet to encourage him to plan for his future. Taylor and the principal met several times daily, and the principal reassured him that he had to step up to the plate and do the work. The principal made a calendar and used stickers to mark off the days to graduation. Of course Taylor thought this was childish; however, he would ask if he got his sticker for the day, and they enjoyed a good laugh.

One day in PE class Taylor was hit playing basketball and broke his nose. Before he would even let the principal contact his mother he asked if leaving was going to prevent him from getting his sticker for the day. He was asking this as blood was dripping from his face and hands.

Taylor's demeanor changed some. He realized the people who cared about him were the ones who were going to stand by him no matter what he chose in life. He did graduate, and it was such an honor to see him get his diploma. He has so much to offer the world. He is likeable, charming, and capable of doing whatever he chooses.

Taylor has so much to look forward to in his future adventures. Even when he chose not to look at the good things and stayed negative, the school staff showered him with care and encouragement. The greatest thing about Taylor is he will make a difference in this world. Of course, Taylor was given his calendar with his stickers at graduation. At this point, Taylor is enrolled in a postsecondary program and is furthering his career. He stops by occasionally to check in and make sure no one has forgotten him.

Behavior strategies that have proven to be effective with the nontraditional education students are the focus of this chapter. The strategies are easily adaptable into any situation working with youth. Personal stories are shared showing the difference made using the strategies.

All these strategies helped empower the students to establish appropriate behavior guidelines and learning patterns. Successful in the nontraditional school, these strategies can easily be used to work with students at risk in other school settings and can be adapted to fit those learning environments.

• 5 •

Connecting the Dots . . .

Social/Community Strategies

No genius ever attributed his or her success to a worksheet.

—Bernadette Donovan and Rose Marie Iovino

$\mathcal{I}$ssues that didn't exist 20 years ago have become solidly integrated in American society. School violence, dissolution of the nuclear family unit, and the role of the federal government have forever altered the landscape of public education. Whether by choice or force, the educators' roles have expanded beyond the instructional realm to incorporate duties normally reserved for parents.

Today's learners are seeking a way to make their lives complete and meaningful, while educators are searching for solutions. The answers lie within the heart of every educator. Individuals who are committed to meeting the needs of all types of learners and are not afraid of taking chances can make an enormous difference in the lives of children. The journey down the yellow brick road does not have to be treacherous; while there might be hazards along the way, strong leadership, collaboration, communication, and a vision for generations of all children mark the path toward excellence.

Recognizing the need for change and breaking away from tradition can create uncertainty and strife within any school setting. Skepticism and hesitation among faculty members can result in turmoil. In general, most people are fearful of change and more comfortable with what is "safe" or "routine." Educators are no exception and are the least likely to alter routines. Incorporating new strategies and veering from traditional classroom management procedures hinges upon several factors. Timing, attitudes, support among school administrators and fellow educators, resources, and practicality are essential components in developing strategies that meet the needs of students.

Friedman (2005) shares an important insight about motivating students:

> The most effective motivational strategy is to appeal explicitly to young people's inherent desire to control their lives. . . . And teachers can design lessons that enhance students' perception of their ability to control behaviors and outcomes . . . learning to control processes and outcomes is more than a means to an end; it's an end in itself. And as students are taught to influence their surroundings and behaviors, they are also taught their other lessons along the way. This motive—the control motive—is an essential tool for teachers trying to engage students in a learning partnership. (p. 71)

The solutions are right before us in the form of caring educators. Nothing can diminish the human spirit when the heart and mind of an educator is determined to empower students.

Many students in today's society are also seeking meaning and completeness in their lives. Instead of viewing themselves as capable students with unlimited resources, they see themselves as outsiders without a place to fit in. Students are searching for missing parts of themselves in order to become productive members of society. In many cases, students are not being taught to look inside of themselves to discover their own capabilities of becoming successful. Instead, the students are mandated to perform as robotic beings targeted to improve the test scores. Unfortunately, today's students are being shuffled through an education system where passing tests and raising test scores are deemed the most important aspects of education in American schools.

Implementing a support system provides security for learners who seek to belong. The support relieves the alienation of the learner and encourages living in this society. Academic and behavior strategies used in the nontraditional education program are provided; however, other supports are needed to help complete the development of the whole child. The strategies and supports do not fall into a specific group, so this chapter is dedicated to providing the extra supports that help students achieve success in life.

The following are examples of extra supports.

GRADUATION COACH/INTERVENTIONIST

The graduation coach serves as a liaison between the base school and the nontraditional school. Each middle and high school has a graduation coach, or interventionist, to provide additional support to the students at risk of dropping out of school. Each graduation coach/interventionist should know each child by name and develop a support system that surrounds those students.

The additional support often includes meeting with the students to discuss academic or behavioral issues, including situations outside of school.

The graduation coaches work closely with the teachers and families to ensure that students' needs are met. Another caring adult will help create the "sense of belonging" that so many at-risk learners need for the extra push toward becoming responsible adults.

Finding an adult other than a teacher or administrator to reach out to in times of need may be all the learners need to get a shot of hope when they become overwhelmed or down in the dumps on a hard day.

MENTORS

Mentors are people who volunteer to spend quality time with other people. School systems across America have incorporated mentors in their schools to help students who need additional support. Mentors are trained and screened. Good mentors establish trust and rapport with students based on interests, goals, and need. Mentors provide students with the positive influence and hope necessary to deal with their problems.

The mentor's role may be playing board games, helping with homework, watching a movie, talking, or even reading. Quality time focused on the student and the student's interests creates a strong bond and additional support to the at-risk learner. Community agencies may provide lists of trained mentors to help students.

COMMUNITIES IN SCHOOLS

Communities in Schools (CIS) has worked closely with the school system by providing services necessary for student achievement. The CIS program is intended to help students stay in school and prepare for life by taking a community-development approach to supporting education. It serves to unify existing resources of communities around children, families, and schools as a support system to help students realize and live up to their potential.

The CIS organization in our community participates in a grant to provide additional services to the nontraditional education program. CIS provides mentors, tutors, college and career readiness activities, job shadowing, college tours, field trips, life skills training, and other services. For example, team-building training, through a local college ropes course, equipped the students with shared responsibilities and trust.

The founder of CIS and author of *The Last Dropout* (2007), Bill Milliken, put it clearly when he said, "CIS helps mold the system around the child rather than forcing the child to fit into the system" (p. 178).

DEVELOP INDEPENDENCE, GROWTH, AND SECURITY (DIGS), INC.

DIGS is a group of parents, caregivers, and concerned citizens who formed a 501C3 nonprofit corporation to "Develop Independence, Growth, and Security" for the adults in the community with developmental disabilities. DIGS, Inc. is located in one of the spare classrooms on the FCEC campus and works with the students. The partnership is a win-win opportunity for both groups.

The FCEC students helped the members of DIGS with making garden art, which was used as a fundraiser in a local festival. The students helped take the wiring out of old chandeliers, put them back together, and paint them. They also helped with making concrete stepping stones. It was beneficial to the students who learned about DIGS and people with disabilities in general. The students asked wonderful questions about different disabilities and abilities. The groups worked well together and served to do away with some old stereotypes about disabilities.

Why is DIGS, Inc., important? It gives adults with disabilities other sources of support at a time when:

- Community services using federal or state funding sources have waiting lists, funding freezes, and complex rules and regulations.
- Choices for finding housing beyond parents' or grandparents' homes are limited and expensive.
- Opportunities are needed for these adults to have leisure choices with others they can truly call *friends.*
- The number of adults with developmental disabilities needing services is increasing each year.

LOCAL AGENCIES

Many students in the nontraditional education program receive outside services such as judicial support, family intervention services, and counseling.

The agencies work closely with the families to provide needed support to help the learners and caregivers stay on track.

Probation officers work closely with the students by making visits to the school. They regularly check attendance, grades, and behavior of students in their care. Connecting with the school encourages the students to follow school guidelines and provide additional support.

FLOYD COUNTY JUVENILE PROBATION

This group of dedicated workers is consistently trying to find proactive interventions to help students. One important factor is to intervene in a positive manner with the intention of steering students toward better lifestyle choices. The court system works closely with all stakeholders to keep students focused on success.

It is amazing how the probation officers teach students how to cope, working behind the scenes not to draw attention to them or their situation. Students are treated with dignity. There is an unprecedented trust level along with an understanding of the importance of compassion and acceptance of others. Students are taught to believe in themselves.

Many strategies are used by the Floyd County Juvenile Probation workers. These include the following:

- *Truancy Treatment Team.* The Truancy Treatment Team began meeting in January of the 2000/2001 school year. The team was charged with the responsibility of reviewing, developing, and contracting with students, parents, and appropriate community agencies a plan to improve excessive absenteeism and tardies. The team consists of members from the Floyd County Board of Education, Rome City Schools, Floyd County Juvenile Court, the District Attorney's Office, Department of Family and Children Services, Department of Juvenile Justice, Floyd County school nurses, and Highland Rivers Behavioral Health workers.
- The Truancy Treatment Team meets every other Tuesday during the school year. The meeting is held with the students and their parents to discuss the attendance issues and to see if the team can offer any services to the family. The team has taken a more firm approach over the past several years but at the same time has been compassionate and aware of each family's issues. The team has made a concerted effort to break down the barriers that prevent children from attending school on a regular and consistent basis.

- The family agrees to send their child to school. If the agreement is broken, school officials refer the family to magistrate court to arrest the parents, or a referral is made to the juvenile court for truancy.
- *Mauldin Pattern Assessments.* Mauldin Pattern Assessment (MPA) measures behavioral patterns, determines risk potentials, and recommends general levels of care for adolescents. The probation staff makes referrals based on the child's needs to local resources, which may include individual or family counseling, anger management, drug and alcohol counseling, and so on.
- *Parental Enrichment Program.* The Parental Enrichment Program (PEP) is a program designed for unruly teens and their parents who are in crisis and need intervention. Eight weekly sessions are led by two therapists focusing on communication, responsibility, problem solving, family relationships, and negotiation.
- *Diversion Program.* Court staff makes referrals to local agencies based on the outcome of the MPA and also on what needs the child has. Probation staff may refer the student to seek mental health services for counseling and drug or alcohol abuse, teen pregnancy, anger management, or other issues.

  The Diversion Program is a program created by the Floyd County Juvenile Court in 2006 to help kids learn from their mistakes and not get caught in the system. The only youth eligible for this program are youth who are first-time misdemeanor offenders (excluding drug-related charges) and score low on a risk assessment.

  If it is determined that a youth does quality for the Diversion Program, he or she is given assignments to complete that are as closely related to the specific charge as possible, such as supervision, fees, community service, the YES program (shoplifting prevention), apology letters, essays, counseling, restitution, and so on. The youth is given about two months to prove he or she is responsible and complete all the conditions of their Diversion Program by the deadline without receiving any new charges. If the youth successfully does all this, the charges are dismissed.
- *School reports.* The court requires juveniles on probation to take school reports completed by the teachers each week. This is a way for the probation officers to communicate with the teachers. The reports include attendance, behavior, and grades of the juveniles.
- *School visits.* Members of the probation staff visit local schools to check on their assigned students. Staff members are able to maintain contact with school officials and get updates. The students can see the probation staff and school staff working together to help the students become successful.

DEPARTMENT OF JUVENILE JUSTICE

The Department of Juvenile Justice (DJJ) provides supervision, detention, and a wide range of treatment and educational services for youth referred to DJJ by the juvenile courts. DJJ provides delinquency prevention services for at-risk youth through collaborative efforts with other public, private, and community entities.

The probation officers not only teach the importance of self-improvement, but they teach the importance of leading others in the way they should go. They let students know about resources and programs that will assist them with behavioral changes. For example, the probation officers address anger management concerns through an anger management component of their program. They are role models who show that the "impossible" is indeed possible.

The Floyd County DJJ consists of two offices, Community Services and Intake (CSI) and High Intensity Team Supervision (HITS). The CSI office provides supervision to youth committed to the DJJ by juvenile court. These youth are supervised in a variety of settings.

Youth may be placed in their homes; relative or nonrelative placements; room, board, and watchful oversight (RBWO) programs (group homes, independent living programs [ILPs], therapeutic foster homes [TFCs], wilderness programs); alcohol or drug (A/D) programs; mental health facilities; regional youth detention centers (RYDCs); or a Youth Development Campus (YDC). All youth are served with a goal of identifying and meeting their individual risk and needs, minimizing the amount of time they are removed from their communities.

The HITS office serves both committed and noncommitted youth. There are two primary types of supervision: HITS and Housebound. The HITS program is a progress level system that includes group attendance, school monitoring, and in-home monitoring. Housebound is an intense monitoring program used for youth awaiting court or as a sanction for violation of supervision by both juvenile court and DJJ-supervised youth. Both CSI and HITS collaborate with the Local Interagency Planning Team (LIPT) to access community resources.

TURNING POINT

One of the most difficult parts of my job is seeing one of our students escorted out of school in handcuffs. I understand the reasons in my head; however, my heart sees the defeated and broken child. Often it is not enough to tell and warn students of the consequences of choosing the "easy" way as opposed to the right way. Sometimes they just have to see it firsthand to know they messed up.

Let me tell you about Ethan. Ethan enrolled in our school during his middle school years. He was assigned to our program because of constant disruption and disturbing the educational process for others. Ethan had been placed on juvenile probation in previous months for being unruly at home. He had appeared in court and was given community service time to complete along with probation.

Ethan had a difficult time with authority of all types. No matter the approach, if a teacher suggested one thing Ethan would do the opposite regardless of the consequences. He was determined to do what he wanted when he wanted, and no one could tell him otherwise.

Ethan had been with us for about four months when I received a call from his probation officer. The officer questioned Ethan's progress in school and attitude toward others. Ethan's grades were low, usually in the mid-70s range. He was capable of much more, but he did not care. He was perfectly content to just do what he wanted. The probation officer shared that Ethan had not completed his community service by the deadline.

You can guess the rest of this story. Ethan was taken away from our school and taken into custody for failure to follow directives of the court. He served several months in the youth detention center. He returned to us to finish his assigned term. It would be wishful thinking to say that this made a change in Ethan's life or that he has grown into a productive young man making good decisions.

That is not the case. Ethan was involved in more crime and is currently serving time in the state prison. Ethan has written to us and shared that prison is so different from youth detention. He shared that if he had known what it was like in the jail, he would definitely have chosen a different path.

The sheriff in the area is proactive toward creating positive youth programs and activities. Part of the Sheriff's Office Youth Initiative, the Turning Point Program utilizes a structured, discipline-based jail environment as well as discussions with inmates to navigate youth toward better decision making.

The Turning Point Program is designed to show students the path that leads to making bad choices and then let them see firsthand the consequences of making bad decisions. It involves taking a trip to the Floyd County Jail for approximately three to four hours to see what lies ahead for those who choose to violate the law. The students are divided into small groups of 10 to 15 each, with boys and girls going separately.

The youth arrive in the booking area and are immediately treated as new inmates. The deputies meet them with the rules and regulations of the jail. Youth are informed of the operations and guidelines to follow while an inmate at the facility. Placed in holding cells, the students are booked in and given identification bracelets and inmate coveralls. No longer are they students; they have become inmates of the system.

Next, the group is given tubs of supplies. They carry these tubs to assigned cells. The tubs include bedding supplies: a sheet, pillow, and blanket for the duration of their time in incarceration. Also included in the tub are hygiene supplies: soap, toothpaste, toothbrush, and shampoo. Inmates are told these supplies are all they get and not to expect anything else.

Carrying their tubs, each inmate is led down the corridors to the assigned cells. Inmates are not allowed to speak to others and must face the wall of the jail when officials walk by. The group is placed in their cell block and locked in the assigned cells. They are to make the bed and put out supplies in a visible area for inspection. All the time they are settling in, deputies are constantly monitoring the process, correcting inappropriate actions.

Once the students have complied with the instructions and are locked in, actual inmates are brought into the block. The inmates go around and try to intimidate the students. The inmates cannot get to the students; however, the students are awakened by the boldness and fierceness of the jail experience. Many of the students end up giving up their tub supplies to the real inmates due to the intimidation. The students are well aware they cannot be touched but still end up handing over their possessions. This experience lasts about 10 to 15 minutes and gets everyone's attention.

The student group is brought out of their cells and instructed to sit on the floor in the block. At this time the real inmates share their experiences with the students to deter the students from incarceration. The inmates share their life as criminals and share personal experiences of how they were consumed by personal desires rather than making good decisions. The inmates' offenses vary: drug charges, assault, theft, and even murder. Many inmates share their desire to go back to the teen years and make better decisions, especially where education is concerned.

The greatest part of the whole experience is for the students to see firsthand the consequences for choices made daily. The inmates tell it like it is in jail. They share the real deal of being an inmate. The group is allowed to ask questions of the inmates.

Deputies then escort the students to tour the jail facilities. It is frightening to see the various cell blocks and hear the doors lock behind each group as they move through the jail. They see inmates grouped in cell blocks according to type and degree of crime. The student group watches from an observation tower used to monitor the cell blocks.

The group sees the lack of privileges in jail and how rights are stripped. For example, it is clear that the shower facilities and bathrooms are monitored as well as the general population area. Watching television is a privilege, with the channel selected by the deputy on duty and only if rules are followed by all inmates.

The student group is then escorted back to their cell block. They go through a question-and-answer session with jail officials. It is interesting to hear the questions asked by the group. Officials recap the visit and make sure the students know how to prevent a real visit. The group is then taken back to booking and released after changing and turning in the ID bracelets.

This is a proactive approach to curtailing crime at an early stage by experiencing incarceration and being stripped of normal, everyday privileges. Turning Point made believers out of many of the students. Behavior changes were immediate, with a new respect and greater understanding of the law. It is a great partnership with the community focused on reducing crime among juveniles.

ANGER MANAGEMENT

The anger management program is designed for those students who have been identified by faculty, parents, or probation officers as exhibiting anger a great deal of the time. These youth either repress those feelings or express them inappropriately. Characteristics that lead to students' participation in the program include when students:

- often have frequent conflicts with friends or family members,
- exhibit oppositional behavior at school,
- have difficulty with authority figures such as teachers,
- are easily provoked,
- often feel angry,
- tend to "bottle up" their feelings,
- have difficulty staying calm when agitated,
- tend to act before thinking,
- have frequent anger outbursts, or
- have difficulty expressing their feelings appropriately.

The focus of the program is to help students understand that anger is often a protective response to a perceived fear or threat. When students feel threatened, their instinct is to survive or protect themselves. That is where anger and aggressiveness come in. The anger management program helps students learn:

- relaxation techniques, such as deep breathing and relaxing,
- techniques for changing the way they think, such as replacing angry thoughts with more rational ones,
- problem-solving techniques to focus on finding a solution,
- better communication skills,
- use of humor to diffuse anger, and
- techniques to change their environment and recognize that it is usually their immediate surroundings that cause their irritation and fury.

Students learn when their anger is harmful versus when it is beneficial, what triggers their anger, how they typically respond when angry and the resulting consequences, and alternate ways for expressing their anger more appropriately.

The students in the anger management group learn with and from peers. The weekly sessions include time to share with each other and help resolve situations the students faced throughout the week. The students learn what does and does not work for them, discussing with their peers and leaders alternate ways to deal with anger issues. Learning to listen and to work together on shared problems helps the students realize they are not alone. Students are also given anger scenarios for the group to resolve.

Derrin was a student who participated in anger management. His anger prevented him from learning because most of his day was spent in isolation away from the other students. Before beginning anger management Derrin had the habit of walking down the hallway with a presence that dared anyone to speak to him. He would often be heard using profanity or challenging other students to "push his buttons" to set him off. Anything that he did not like or want to do would result in a confrontation. Derrin had the mindset that he could do whatever he wanted to do because he had always been able to bully everyone.

After several sessions, Derrin began to enjoy his time in anger management. To him it was a time he could be out of the classroom. He began to actively participate in the sessions and share his true feelings, realizing others were like him. Anger management was something that Derrin actually looked forward to. He made much progress in the group. He loved expressing his anger through drawing—showing the negative and positive side of behavior.

After successfully completing anger management, Derrin left the session and was walking down the hall with his certificate in hand. One of the teachers asked to see his certificate. His reply was that he had just finished anger management. A student in the class said something about the certificate that offended Derrin. Derrin looked at the teacher and said he needed to go back and start the second session of anger management. Success!

LAW AND YOU

Middle school and high school students often do not have the understanding that what they choose to do now could affect the remainder of their lives. Many have been involved with the juvenile justice system and believe that whatever they do will soon be forgotten. With this in mind, law enforcement officials, probation officers, and district attorney staff come into the school and share with students about laws and the consequences of breaking the laws. They speak frankly and directly to students concerning choices. The students are active participants in the discussion. Laws about drugs and drinking are usually the two main areas of concern for students. Question-and-answer time results in questions about dropping out of school, driver's license guidelines, and the age to move out of their parents' home.

Many students also want to know about unruly child laws, dating and rape issues, and even gun control. Personal issues the students are facing are sometimes brought up that allow for a group sharing of experiences. Students can also speak to the presenters after the presentation and ask specific questions about something they may be facing.

COMMUNITY INVOLVEMENT

The students are encouraged to take an active role in activities and events in the local community. As mentioned in chapter 2, service learning is a key to connecting academics with real-life experiences. While students are active in completing service projects, participation in other events is also encouraged. Events have included the following:

- The students, along with the 100 Black Men of Rome, sponsored a book signing at the Barnes and Noble bookstore. It featured Judge Marvin Arrington's book entitled *Making My Mark*. The book signing was in conjunction with the Black History Month celebration. Judge Arrington has family ties to Rome and has made his mark in Georgia.
- Faculty and staff members, along with students, participated in a "Teen Expo" at the local Boys and Girls Club. It was a community-based event focused on teens, with special events and activities to promote healthy choices. An FCEC display showed the value of education and student achievement and shared FCEC programs. Free books were also given to youth.

- Faculty, staff, and students helped with a carwash to raise money for students to attend a state conference sponsored by the 100 Black Men of Rome.
- The Commission on Children and Youth, along with state representative Katie Dempsey, invited FCEC students to participate in a "Teen Table Talk Forum." The event included teens from all sectors of the community and allowed students to share concerns about being a teen in today's society.
- Mr. Alan Smith, commander of the VFW Post 4911, presented a flag to the school and discussed patriotism and the meaning of the flag in a ceremony attended by the students and staff.
- The students participated in the Kroger Corporation collection of coats to be given away to needy people in the community.
- Cosmetologists from local salons visited the school and spent time with the students discussing the importance of hair care and maintenance. Many students showed an interest in pursuing this avenue as a career.
- Community groups sponsored a Boys 2 Men breakfast. The male students could invite an adult male who had been a positive role model.
- A breakfast was hosted by community sponsors for the female students. Each female could invite an adult female who had been a positive role model.
- Jay Asher, author of *Thirteen Reasons Why*, visited the school and discussed his book. He answered questions and led discussions with the students and staff.

Students have worked closely with other agencies and community events such as the local fair exhibits and festivals. Members of the community drop by the school and visit with the students during lunch or break. It is important for the students to respond to the needs of those around them. Many students have never explored opportunities within the community. By participating in events, students witness the opportunities that are available locally.

MEDIA

Educating students in the twenty-first century requires taking teaching in a new direction. A class of students 30 years ago would have to spend countless hours inside a library with encyclopedias researching information that today's learner can find at the touch of a button in a mere fraction of the time. Inquisitive minds develop according to the way information is learned. Students today are not satisfied with just learning facts but want to delve into "why" and "how" these facts came into being. Methods of media use have played a major role in raising our students to discover the many facts that were not so readily available years ago. The youth of today have been raised with the world at the touch of a button. Yet the styles and strategies of educating students have not really advanced to meet the needs of this generation of students.

There has been much research about the impact of the media on our children. Most of the information paints a negative, dismal outlook about the way violence is portrayed in video games, movies, music venues, and other types of electronic devices that were not around a generation ago. Rock stars send messages of gang affiliation. Movies show sexual promiscuity, and teen magazines show models that send the message that you have to dress and look a certain way to be popular. Pornography is easily displayed on the Internet with little or no monitoring restrictions. Multitudes of websites are opening communication with unknown faces to entice young students into meetings outside the safety net of watchful guardians. And the list goes on and on.

But is all media bad? Kids today are entering school with a wealth of knowledge and experiences through the use of the media. World events are a click away using the Internet. Troops in various countries are emailing students with firsthand accounts of combat. Cell phones make it possible to talk to others all over the world. The media today presents students with an actual here-and-now mode of communication and thinking.

Don Tapscott, author of several books related to the digital revolution, states that our generation of young people is more technologically advanced than most of the adults. This is due to their exposure in their early years. In his book *Growing Up Digital* (1999), he reports:

> The people, companies and nations which succeed in the new economy will be those who listen to their children. We can listen to their views on the world. We can learn from their effortless mastery and applications of new tools. (p. 13)

Regardless of the media and the influence it has on today's youth, it is important to remember one important detail—it is here to stay. No matter what people think about its influences, technology is constantly changing and emerging with new devices that are in high demand among young people.

This chapter provides information on the extra support services provided in the nontraditional education program, from graduation coaches and mentors to various outside agencies that provide assistance and guidance for at-risk learners. Personal student stories are also shared in this chapter.

Beyond Brick and Mortar

Parent Strategies

*If you want children to keep their feet on the ground, put some respon-
sibility on their shoulders.*

—Abigail Van Buren

To what extremes are we willing to go as a society to prepare our children
for the realities of daily life? Sadly, the world we knew 10 years ago has
completely changed. Today's world is one of frailness and uncertainty. The
first generations post 9/11 are either college bound or already entering the
upperclassmen years. For these students, the cruelties of life have hit home in
a dramatic way. While these generations have been rudely introduced to the
realities of hate and terrorism, the students in today's classroom are exposed
daily to the side effects of issues plaguing our nation.

Traditionally, school districts have been perceived as places of learning;
over the past 15 years, the definition and expectation of what services school
districts should provide have been completely altered. The implementation
of federal food service programs to provide free breakfasts to needy students
and services to those who are considered homeless have greatly expanded the
definition of the responsibilities of American schools. Why have these types
of federal initiatives been implemented in our schools? The answer is simple:
the continued financial decline of the American economy.

As a nation, we have yet to recover from the 2008 recession, and as
of 2011, the future continues to look bleak. Where does that leave us as
educators in regard to serving our student populations? How has the face of
what traditionally constituted the American family changed? These are just
a couple of questions that educators are wrestling with daily. However, the
critical question is this: how can we provide our students' families with the
support they need?

HOT OR COLD

Efforts to make every person entering a school building feel welcome should be a priority among all school members. Schools should serve as a haven not only for school leaders, teachers, and students but for parents, caregivers, and community members as well. The saying "You only get one chance to make a good first impression" is certainly relevant to how people might ultimately perceive a school when they first enter a school building.

Every educator should ask the question: is my school "hot" or "cold"? In many respects, a school is a living, breathing entity and projects the energy of all school members. When any member of the community, whether a business partner, parent, guardian, or general visitor, enters the school, the environment should be one of warmth, happiness, and productivity.

It's simple: a school should serve as a place people feel welcome and valued. We are all very busy with the stresses associated with providing school members with the services and support needed daily; it is easy to for us to forget how far a kind word or hearty welcome goes in making people feel valued.

Creating a welcoming environment requires a commitment to being pursuable and attentive to the needs of all individuals. The faculty and staff at the FCEC have made the process of making all people feel welcome into an art. Since its inception, the program members have strived to create an environment where all are embraced regardless of ethnicities, cultural differences, and social issues. Many have described the FCEC as being a place that instantly feels like home the minute one walks through the door. In fact, the program has often been deemed a "second home" to everyone.

Caregivers and parents are responsible for transporting their children to and from school; however, bus transportation is available to the students. While for some the financial cost of transporting their student can be somewhat of a hardship, the situation actually provides a unique opportunity for the students' families and FCEC members. By having the students dropped off and picked up each day, FCEC members and families have an opportunity to develop solid relationships. The caregivers and parents are able to see the school in action and to be actively involved in their children's educations.

By promoting a caring school climate and empowerment, FCEC members have built a strong commitment to open communication and empowerment. Responses from surveys completed by caregivers and parents over the years have indicated that the atmosphere at the nontraditional education center is exceptional, receptive, and very empathetic to the issues the students face. Often, it is simply the encouragement and the time given to listen that makes the difference with people.

Defining the difference between a "hot" and "cold" school is quite simple. Schools that are considered "hot" openly welcome everyone; the environment is built around mutual respect and shared interest in sustaining an atmosphere of hopefulness. At one time or another, we have all received poor service in a restaurant. Perhaps it was overly crowded or there were issues going on in the kitchen. It may have seemed like it took forever to be served or that the wait staff seemed uninterested in providing quality service.

Schools that are considered "cold" are similar to the wait staff in a poorly managed restaurant. The lack of interest, support, and attention to the needs of school members is similar to that of a wait staff that neglects their duties. Schools that exhibit characteristics of being "cold" often lack morale and the support needed to generate an environment conducive to members being able to blossom.

Characteristics of "Hot" Schools

- The "energy" generated from the positivity of school members is evident upon entering the facility.
- School members are genuinely concerned about the students and their family members.
- School members (students, parents, and teachers) openly express love and pride associated with being part of the school. Simply stated, the students and other school members love their school!
- Everyone is openly welcomed upon entering the building.
- Morale is positive and generally determined to be at a high level among school members.
- School members on all levels openly support the efforts of one another.
- Opportunities for growth are provided and encouraged among school members.
- Hope and belief: school members have a clear vision of hope for a bright future; they truly believe all students can achieve and be successful.

Characteristics of a "Cold" School

- There is a lack of support from community and school members.
- Low morale among school members results in a sense of loss and frustration.

- Feelings of frustration and anger arise associated with not being able to correct underlying issues.

Strategies toward Building a "Hot" School

- *Stop, look, and listen.* What are the needs of school members? One of the biggest mistakes educators can make singlehandedly is to assume they know what is best for the school. Remember, there is always more than one angle to the situation. Often, educators only see a certain side to a situation; they fail to recognize how others perceive what is occurring in the school. Stopping to take the time to listen to the needs of school members cannot be overstressed. By truly paying attention to what is being said, issues can be properly identified and a plan can be developed to address areas that need improvement.
- *Utilize outside resources.* Local businesses and even chain restaurants are often eager to provide coupons as incentives for students. Initiating a relationship with businesses and actively involving them within the school can be a wonderful opportunity to gain resources.

TAKING CARE OF OUR OWN

Similar to many small towns across the United States, the failure of local businesses has led to higher levels of unemployment within the school district. This economic condition has created a new wave of people needing government assistance. The district recently experienced a significant increase in the number of students who qualify for the federal free and reduced lunch program, with a 60 percent participation rate. The need for school employees to be aware of available community resources cannot be understated in this day and time.

There are many wonderful organizations and community resources available to assist struggling families. Local food pantries hosted by area churches can be a valuable outreach service. Additionally, organizations such as the local Lion's Club can assist in acquiring eyewear for needy children. It is not unusual to see staff members of the FCEC assisting family members in completing applications for the local food pantry or emergency relief funds.

While completing job applications and developing résumés may be an easy task for many people, for certain individuals it is a nightmare. A few years ago, a single mother with a child enrolled in the FCEC desperately needed assistance in developing a résumé and preparing for a job interview.

Comfortable with the staff members, she candidly asked for assistance with prepping for the job. Landing the position would be a huge opportunity for the parent, and she truly needed the income the job would generate.

The parent was provided with the advice and preparation she needed for the interview; however, there was one small issue. Unfortunately, the mother had been out of the workforce for some time and was experiencing severe financial difficulties. The parent lacked the funds to purchase new clothing and a much-needed hairstyling. One of the FCEC members graciously offered to cover the costs of the needed items and personal care.

There have been times when parents have felt like they had nowhere to turn, and FCEC members have stepped forward over the years to meet the needs of those who have asked for assistance. A couple of years ago, a parent who was recently divorced and living several thousand miles away from relatives experienced a medical emergency. Alone in a town where she hardly knew anyone other than the school staff who had been working with her sons, the parent contacted the staff members for assistance.

Two of the staff members rushed to the hospital, attended to her needs, and upon her release escorted her home. Over the next couple of weeks, the two staff members transported her to the doctor for checkups. While the FCEC staff members were not obligated to take personal time to assist the parent, they understood the connection between school, parent, and student.

Who would have imagined 15 years ago that our economy would have been in such a dire situation? Without a doubt, the financial situation within the United States has created a generation of children who are growing up in a world of fear and uncertainty. The children are victims, and the economic downturn has hit way too close to home. Each day, students are coming to school hungry and uncertain as to where they will sleep that night.

Sadly, in the FCEC this scenario had been occurring long before the financial crisis of 2008. A few years ago, we had a student named Eric enrolled in the program. Eric often came to school dirty and unkempt. He would lay his head on the desk and sleep for the entire day despite the pleading from teachers to wake up. One day, as Eric was entering the school building, Dr. Allee, who happened to be standing in the front office greeting students, looked down and saw that he did not have any shoes on. The student was standing in his socks, intent on going about his day without shoes. Shocked and baffled, Dr. Allee calmly asked Eric where his shoes were. Without hesitation, Eric responded, "My brother has them, I lent them to him to wear to school today so they won't make fun of him today."

Dr. Allee privately asked Eric to sit in the office waiting area as she discreetly slipped into my office. Teary-eyed and distraught over the student not having any shoes to wear, she explained what was going on with Eric and his lack of shoes. We quickly sprang into action with a plan to provide Eric shoes to wear to class so that his classmates would not know the student was in such a dire situation. Without Eric knowing what was occurring, I quickly ran home and "borrowed" a brand-new pair of my husband's tennis shoes.

Thankfully, my home is not far from the school, and I was able to retrieve the new shoes before the first bell rang for class. Luckily, Eric and my husband shared the same shoe size. The student was extremely grateful for the shoes. As we quizzed Eric on what was going on at home, we learned that he and his family were currently sleeping in a car, and occasionally they would rent a seedy hotel room. By taking the time to develop a relationship with the students and reaching out to them beyond the classroom, we were able to earn the trust of the student.

Eric was a very quiet student who never knew anything other than difficulties in life. We were able obtain much-needed services for the family through the school social worker. As the semester progressed, Eric began to improve academically and socially. However, due to constantly moving and years of instability within the home, he had tremendous gaps academically. We discovered that he enjoyed repairing engines on small items such as lawnmowers and motorcycles.

A deal was struck with Eric that if he worked hard in the classroom, time would be provided for him to work on small motors. The staff members brought in or solicited friends and family for old lawnmowers in need of repair. The strategy was successful with Eric, and he responded positively to the incentive. Preparing our students for tomorrow goes beyond the textbook and certainly beyond a standardized test. Eric is a prime example of how one has to step beyond the classroom door to best meet the needs of a student.

It is extremely difficult to see families within the community struggle to the point of having nowhere else to turn than to the school for assistance. A school has a wealth of resources, and often people are unaware of the services a school employee can provide by serving as a liaison between school and community outreaches. Clearly, the needs of families must be met; whereas schools in the past served only to provide academics, the roles and expectations have changed.

FAMILIES TODAY

When I entered the teaching profession 29 years ago, the face of the American family was quite different from what is being seen in schools today. While the divorce rate in America was beginning to climb and women were entering the workforce in greater numbers, a traditional nuclear unit was typical in the community where I taught. The father was the breadwinner, whereas the mother stayed at home and occasionally volunteered at school. While this was perceived as the ideal American family 29 years ago, the realities of individual family roles have changed considerably. I have seen a great deal of change in regard to family structure and education over the years, but the trends that have been occurring over the past 10 years are quite unsettling.

Roughly eight years ago, the faculty and staff began to notice a significant change in regard to who was raising the students being served in the program. Whereas the teachers were accustomed to teaching children of divorced parents, an alarming pattern among the student population began to emerge. Instead of being raised by a natural parent, a significant portion of the student body was being cared for by extended family members.

Over the years, the students were being raised by single mothers. Where were the fathers? Typically, the fathers were incarcerated and completely out of the picture. A strange thing began to occur over the course of eight years. Mothers were no longer in the picture, and often they were also incarcerated. Suddenly, the staff members found themselves in a new situation in regard to dealing with parents and students.

The question "Who is raising these children?" resounded among the staff members. The answer to this question could be found on the shoulders of grandmothers and aunts of students. The job of raising teenagers is a challenge for the most alert parent; however, caring for a chronically unruly youth is at best extremely difficult.

Over the years, the FCEC staff members continually heard disheartening stories of elderly grandmothers trying to raise the children of their sons or daughters. Often, the grandmothers were sick, frail, and financially strapped, and the job of attending to just the physical needs of the children was overwhelming. The grandmothers, and in some cases the aunts, were exhausted and overwhelmed with trying to keep the home afloat and the children out of trouble. Frequently, the children the relatives were caring for constantly stayed in trouble with local law enforcement. It was a losing battle for the relatives, and they were beyond any hope of trying to save the troubled children from getting into further trouble with the justice system.

The FCEC faculty and staff have always empathized with the relatives of students and understand the toll incarceration can have on families. Over the years, they have dealt firsthand with the impact of teaching students whose parents are serving sentences. These experiences have led to the program developing strategies to assist both students and their families. The poor choices of natural parents can be detrimental. There are strategies that can be taken to address the situation of parental incarceration.

Strategies for Relatives Raising Nonnatural Children

- *Open-ended discussions.* Discussing the unpleasantries of why the parent(s) are not in the daily life of the child is important. Based upon the age and maturity of the teen, discuss the reasons why the parent(s) are not an active part of their lives at this time. Secrets can be dangerous and create anxiety with anyone, but for a teenager they often lead to blame. The uncanny thing about secrets is that they rarely remain silent and are always discovered. Relatives should ardently strive to develop open-ended relationships where children feel comfortable with asking difficult questions.
- *Support.* Please do not ever hesitate to ask for help! Perhaps a trusted family friend, church minister, or members of a community group could assist in dealing with issues associated with teenagers. There are a great deal of available resources, such as the Boys and Girls Clubs of America, that specialize in providing this type of assistance. Local churches are a fantastic resource for families. Getting teenagers involved in a church with an active youth ministry can deter them from associating with negative influences.
- *Counseling.* The loss of a parent is overwhelming, and the absence can trigger bouts of depression. There are many wonderful counselors who specialize in dealing with teenagers. Do the research! Local churches, schools, and other organizations can recommend a great match for the teenager.
- *Information.* Keeping school members abreast of the situation can be a very effective strategy in supporting the teenager in the home and school settings. Often, behavior exhibited at home is also occurring at school. By working together and communicating on a regular basis, relatives and school members are able to develop a strong support network for the teenager.
- *Fun.* Do something just because! While the thought of having to be seen with a relative might be anguishing to a teenager, the truth is he or she wants to be included in family events. There are all kinds of inexpensive or even free events taking place in your community. Check local newspapers or websites to learn more about dates and events going on in your area.
- *Doing what is best.* The decision to seek outside assistance can be very difficult. Some people may view it as a failure, but the truth is there is

no shame in asking for help. The tragedy lies in not reaching out to obtain needed resources.

PARENTING A TEENAGER

Every parent wants his or her children to become successful in life, to be independent and healthy adults. I remember when my children were small. Watching them try to accomplish simple tasks, it was difficult to stand by and observe. Learning to ride a bicycle was a big undertaking. As a mother, I made sure the helmet was secure and the child had enough clothes to pad a fall should it occur. Watching the determination in their faces as their feet pushed the pedals, only to see them fall, was tough. I would sway back and forth as if I could straighten the wheels to make the ride easier and keep them from falling.

After much trial and error and many bumps and bruises, the task of riding the bike became easier as they learned to manage and control the needed balance. All tasks are not that simple. And it is not easy to watch your children learn hard lessons through pain and failure. The reward, however, is seeing the drive and determination in the eyes of the child when the job is accomplished! The child's accomplishment is a lesson showing that hard work and sticking to a task are worth the risks. Learning this builds self-esteem and gives the children a strong sense of self-worth.

Many parents want to rescue their children from facing disappointments, failures, and rejections. It would be wonderful if students could breeze through school and life never having to experience anything negative. Failures occur often and should be viewed as teachable moments. Learning how to cope with adversities and shortcomings is a life skill essential for every child's overall development. The pitfall is often the reactions of the adults when these events occur.

Instead of helping the child learn to deal with negative experiences, parents may want to step in and save the day. Parents want to believe in their children when a mistake is made; however, many parents want to rescue their children from any fault or blame for negative choices. For instance, imagine a child gets into trouble at school for cheating and goes home and shares his or her version of the incident.

The parent goes to the school and makes excuses that the teacher "doesn't like my child" or "is just picking on my child." The parent is enabling the child to continue the cheating behavior and not making the child responsible for the infraction. The child has won a major battle at home and learned to redirect blame to others rather than learn a valuable life lesson.

David Wilmes, author of the book *Parenting for Prevention* (1995), gives a great definition of the term *enabling* in the following statement: "Enabling is a process whereby well-meaning parents unwittingly allow and even encourage irresponsible and self-destructive behavior in their children by shielding them from the consequences of their actions" (p. 9).

The children of enabling parents are master manipulators. In other words, any negative situation experienced by the child is usually blamed on someone else. The student manipulates the parent into believing that the child is a victim and not responsible for anything that happened. The enabling parent intervenes and takes control of the situation to make sure the child is protected at all costs. This creates major chaos and usually results in a child who is totally dependent on the parent to right the wrong.

The child is not held accountable; therefore, no coping skills are learned. With no experience in accountability, children continue to create chaotic situations, often as attention-getting behaviors. Parents continue to make excuses for the wrong against their children. Many of these children experience low self-esteem that could lead to very negative adult experiences and result in criminal behavior.

The following 12 rules, titled "How to Raise a Juvenile Delinquent" (unpublished), were issued by the Archdeacon of Chesterfield, England. The list was provided to parishioners as a guide to raising children.

1. Begin in infancy to give the child everything he wants. In this way he will grow up to believe that the world owes him a living.
2. When he picks up bad words, laugh at him. It will encourage him to pick up "cuter phrases" that will blow the top of your head off later.
3. Never give him any spiritual training. Wait until he is 21 and then let him decide for himself.
4. Avoid the use of the word "wrong". It may develop a guilt complex. This will condition him to believe later when he is arrested for stealing a car that society is against him and he is being persecuted.
5. Pick up everything he leaves lying around—books, shoes, and clothes. Do everything for him so he will be experienced in throwing the responsibility onto others.
6. Let him read any printed matter he can get his hands on. Be careful the silverware and drinking glasses are sterilized, but let his mind feed on garbage.
7. Quarrel frequently in the presence of the children. Then they won't be shocked when the home is broken up.
8. Give the child all the spending money he wants. Never let him earn his own. Why should he have things as tough as you had them?

9. Satisfy his every craving for food, drink, and comfort. See that every desire is gratified. Denial may lead to harmful frustration.
10. Take his part against the neighbors, teachers, and policemen. They are all prejudiced against your child.
11. When he gets into real trouble, apologize for yourself by saying, "I never could do anything with him."
12. Prepare for a life of grief—you will have it!

Establishing positive and effective working relationships is crucial when working with at-risk learners and their caregivers. Caregivers may include the parent, guardian, grandparent, or significant adult responsible for the primary care of the student. Approximately 5.4 million children live with grandparents in America, according to the 2000 U.S. Census. Many social issues have created diverse family dynamics for children today.

The mindset of the caregiver is one of the most influential factors in the attitude of the learner; therefore, it is critical to include the caregiver in the educational process of the student. Upon enrollment in the nontraditional education program a conference is required for the learner and caregiver. The meeting emphasizes that it takes 100 percent support from all for the student to be successful. Student, caregiver, and educators each contribute 33 ⅓ percent to the equation. If one part of the equation fails, then no one succeeds.

Today's society is riddled with so much diversity in the family unit. A single-parent family where one parent is completely absent creates difficulties for the sole caregiver of the family. Often the single caregiver has the total financial and parental responsibilities for the maintenance and survival of the entire family. Raising children is not only stressful for this caregiver but can also be frustrating.

Structure in the home is crucial to providing smooth transitions for the role of the caregiver, especially for at-risk students. With homework, housework, and providing food and shelter, the caregiver can become overwhelmed and exhausted. The lack of structure enables the children to take advantage of weak moments in the caregiver. The children may suffer because often the caregiver loses authority and no boundaries are maintained within the home. An additional stress for the caregiver is when the child faces structure and boundaries in the educational environment and cannot manipulate the adults. Usually, rebellion and defiance occur and discipline issues hinder the learning process.

When I was growing up, my parents never served as my lawyer, mediator, or banker. If I made a bad decision, I suffered the consequences. If I wanted something special, I worked to earn the money to buy it. I was taught to honor commitments and tell the truth at all times. And most of all I learned respect and developed my self-esteem through hard work. This brings me to an issue that rubs me the wrong way. When did self-esteem become a topic of teaching? Self-esteem is not taught but earned by each individual. Educators are doing our students a disservice by not letting them learn from their mistakes.

Another type of family diversity is blended families. A blended family consists of a parent, stepparent, and children from previous relationships. In essence it is two families "blended" into one household. Children in blended family households can receive additional support from the other natural parent not living in the home. Parents of at-risk children in blended families need to work collaboratively with setting and supporting boundaries in meeting the needs of the children. The children will manipulate the adults if the parents do not work together.

If parents fail to work together, confusion and chaos will ensue for the at-risk learner both at home and school. If given the opportunity, the at-risk learners will play parents against each other and play on sympathies instead of learning to be responsible for choices made. Children of blended families work well when both parents work together to create guidelines and responsibilities for the children wherever the children are located. For example, both parents should establish a curfew for the child to be home that is the same at both houses, not a later time at one house. The same goes with privileges and consequences. Parents should work together to create a unified approach to dealing with children's issues so the children cannot manipulate parents against each other.

Many of our youth today drop out of school simply because they cannot relate to school. Just ask the youth why they drop out of school. Take the time to listen to what they are telling us! Students are not able to explore the avenues to incorporate and expand knowledge on a world-wide level in many academic courses. Although many courses may include some type of research to accompany a lesson or topic, students are hindered from taking the information and creating a connection that shows relevance.

Kevin came to the nontraditional alternative program because he violated the zero-tolerance policy at his traditional school. Kevin was almost to the point of being introverted and insecure, lacking any self-confidence. He showed very little interest in completing assignments and would sink into periods of deep depression. During one of his classes he shared with the teacher that he was taking guitar lessons. The teacher immediately took an interest in Kevin's pursuit of learning the guitar and would talk to him often about his progress. After a few weeks, Kevin brought his guitar to play for the teacher after school one day. This was a huge step for Kevin. Several times

Kevin played the guitar for the teacher, and she was very impressed at how quickly he was learning.

Kevin's mother was very active in his education and would often check to see his progress toward getting his assignments complete. She shared with us about how much Kevin was enjoying his guitar. She even turned a room in their home into a studio for his friends to jam with Kevin. Kevin shared videos of his jam sessions with members of the staff.

Kevin made a special video for a presentation used at a conference that showed his jam sessions. He even wrote special arrangements for the video. Kevin graduated and plans to get married soon. His attitude changed when a teacher took an interest in Kevin as an individual and not just a student. Realizing the need for everyone to work together is crucial for the learners to succeed.

This chapter wraps up the purpose of the book by challenging every reader to focus on empowering the learners to never give up on their dreams and goals. It shows how the nontraditional education program made a difference in the lives of students.

• 7 •

Running on Empty

Voices of Student Success

The only thing worse than being blind is having sight with no vision.

—Helen Keller

𝒥magine for a moment that each student within your school is like a pearl. The student is encased in a protective shell through the school years. Each bit of information is collected and becomes part of the knowledge base of the learner. With the passing of years, the child collects more and more information, building toward a future determined by the individual choices of the student. The protective shell represents all the adults in the student's circle of influence who looks out for the best interest of the child. As the student physically matures and grows, so do the influences.

Each day in the Floyd County Education Center is a new opportunity for the faculty and students to make a positive difference. Being placed in an alternative school program does not necessarily mean a student will continue the pattern of making negative decisions. In fact, the majorities of the students learn from their mistakes, continue on with their education, and become productive citizens. The events leading up to students being assigned to an alternative school program are a result of chronic home and school issues.

The step toward providing students with the skills to become assiduous adults involves identifying and addressing specific issues. Actually helping students involves rolling up the sleeves and sheer determination to not ever give up on them. A former student, Cara Dillard, wrote in a writing assignment, "We all excel—we do not fail; for if one falls short—we all do." This became the motto of the nontraditional education. It is imperative to care about the students. Take the time to know where each student comes from outside of school. Very few educators care only about the four walls of the classroom.

Each morning our staff is at the door, greeting each student by name, establishing a welcoming school environment that focuses on the students. One staff member even sings to the students as they sign in for the day. The students may act like it bothers them; however, if the staff member is absent they want to know who is going to sing and when he is going to be back. Former students even recall their songs when we see them.

The FCEC serves as a safe haven for our students whether they are currently enrolled or have been here previously. This is evident in the continuing contact with those students who have served their assigned time and left. We have former students who come by to visit quite often and others who correspond through emails, cards, and letters. Many drop by to share successes of how they are making a difference. Students graduating from high school, college, and training programs drop by to show off their achievements. We have had former students who leave the hospital after having children and come to our school to show off their new family.

Many students who get new jobs or plan to get married will stop by to let us share in the excitement. Several have joined the military and come by to show off their uniforms and certificates. Students who need advice come by for help in making tough decisions. Some of our students have been arrested for various offenses and come by to apologize for not making good decisions. They do not want any of us to be upset with them. Good news or bad news, the students have kept us in their lives because our staff has been influential by caring about the individuals.

Our staff has reached out to the students by being available to them. When students were involved in accidents, many of our staff members were at the hospital to help and support the families. One student's parent was killed in a tragic accident, and she wanted members of the staff to go in with her for support to see the deceased parent.

Another former student was hospitalized for taking medication not prescribed to him. He was semiconscious and would not talk to his parents, friends, or the doctors treating him. When one of the teachers went to the hospital, she told him "Wake up, we have Biology work to do." His eyes flashed open, and he told her exactly what happened. This was due to the trust and assurance given by this teacher to him when he was in her class. He even cried when she had to leave the hospital. We have had students show up at school without shoes. Staff members quickly provided shoes by purchasing them personally. These are just a very few of the many things the staff at our nontraditional education center has done for the students.

The staff shows support and caring by attending functions outside of school in which the students participate. Whether it is a sporting, church, or other social event, many members of our staff will attend. Relationships are established by taking an interest in the things that interest the students. One staff member has gone to watch students at a local skate park, while others have attended baptisms and Eagle Scout ceremonies. Many times the staff will also attend court hearings that involve our students or their families. Whatever is important to the students becomes important to us. Students need to see that the adults in their lives care about their interests outside of school.

Brandon was a former student who attended our school on two different occasions for various behavior reasons. He needed a very structured environment where he could redirect his intense energy and enthusiasm. Many would describe him as hyper and outspoken. He stuck to his views and would not be swayed by logic or rules. One example was when he challenged the dress code established by our school.

Brandon could not understand why students were not allowed to wear shorts but girls could wear skirts. After explaining to him that the policy did not specify that girls only could wear skirts, I believed the issue was put to rest and he was satisfied with the explanation. The next day Brandon and a few other male students showed up in skirts!

Dr. Amy Allee, our science teacher, quickly took Brandon under her wing. She provided extra duties for Brandon to help with his energetic spirit and need for leadership. He would organize her science materials, run errands, and do just about anything to help her at school. Brandon would come in early or stay after school to help Dr. Allee set up for her science classes. Dr. Allee became his "mom" at school. Brandon lived with an aunt who had raised him from early childhood, and she appreciated the extra help and support that Dr. Allee and our staff provided.

One afternoon when Brandon was working, Dr. Allee talked to him about his future goals and dreams. Brandon had not decided his intentions for after high school, except he kept telling her he was never leaving our school. Dr. Allee often discussed his leadership abilities and need for structured discipline. She suggested he talk with a military recruiter. This was arranged.

Upon graduation Brandon joined the U.S. Marines and headed off for boot camp. After graduation his first stop was at our school in uniform. Dr. Allee has been in constant contact since he enlisted three years ago. She has made sure he not only had the supplies he needed but has provided care packages consistently. Dr. Allee even got him an iPod and filled it with his favorite music while he was on driving details during his time away. He has served in Afghanistan on one tour and is currently deployed overseas at an undisclosed location.

Each time he returns to the United States he makes a point of finding Dr. Allee and making sure she knows his progress. Brandon has presented Dr. Allee with service medals he has earned. When possible he contacts Dr.

Allee on each holiday, even on Mother's Day. He visits the school each time and shares his experiences with the students and staff.

Brandon regularly sends emails when he can to keep us posted on his adventures. It has been a great experience for everyone involved. Brandon is now a corporal and has chosen to stay in the marines until he retires. Last fall, when Brandon returned home for a visit he came out to the alternative school for a visit and to bring a dozen roses for the school secretary, the ISS paraprofessional, and each female teacher. The male teachers were additionally provided with a token of appreciation.

Brandon's story is just one of many examples that show how caring our educators are. They have tremendous impact on our students by developing relationships of trust and care for the students. Several of our students have joined the military and are now serving to make this world better than they found it.

REFLECTIONS FROM THE CLASSROOM

Teacher Story 1

I have known Alyson all of her life—not really on a personal level, but because I had grown up with her mom and ran into them from time to time. I was very surprised when she was sent to my school for possession of pills. When she first came to our school, she had an attitude that no one really cared about her so she was going to do whatever she wanted. I had her in class three times a day so we became close and she felt she could confide in me.

Since I had a good relationship with her mom, I felt it was like working with someone in my own family. Alyson and I had a good teacher-student relationship. She and I would often discuss how she ended up making the choices she had made that caused her to end up at our school and what she needed to do when she was able to return to her home school.

Alyson was always a good student when it came to academics and never had any problems with her schoolwork. Her main problem was always her self-esteem and, I believe, her self-worth. She did not have a good relationship with her father, and she resented that. Her mother really wanted what was best for her but had made some bad choices in her own life that she didn't want Alyson to repeat.

In the beginning, Alyson made some very bad choices by hanging out with kids she had met at our school. She was involved in destructive behavior that was hurting her outside of school. When I learned about what she was doing, I began talking to her and her mom about the importance of keeping some of her old friends who were good influences on her. While working with Alyson we talked often about how great it would be to go back to her home school and be with her friends. After a little while, and spending time with me in class talking about what she really needed to be doing, Alyson came to realize that the choices she was making were not the ones that would get her back to her home school and began to make changes in her life for the better.

Alyson and I talked often, not just at school but outside of school when I would talk to her mom. At the end of her time at our school, I felt Alyson had really grown as a young lady and was maturing in such a way that she could make some better choices once she returned to her home school. The summer after she left our school she became involved in a summer camp at a local college. The camp is a Christian-based college, and it really helped Alyson work on her self-esteem and become a more confident person. She really enjoys the camp and has attended it for two years.

When she returned to her home school, she joined the chorus because she really loves to sing. This was such a good choice for her and she really seemed to enjoy it. During the first few weeks of high school, Alyson called me to let me know she had been nominated for Homecoming Representative for the freshman class. She asked me if I would come to see her in the pageant. I did go and made sure I spoke with her afterward.

Alyson was so excited that I came to see her, and I was proud that she involved me in that part of her life. She is also on the honor roll at her school now. Again, she always did well academically for me, but that she has carried this with her to high school is really great to know.

Alyson and I keep in touch, and she always lets me know how she is doing in school and even called me a few weeks ago to invite me to a party for her mom that is coming up. She also called me recently to let me know she has been chosen for Homecoming Representative again for her sophomore year. I plan to go and watch her in this pageant as well. She is a beautiful, sweet young lady and seems to have found that self-esteem that she was lacking in when I first met her at my school.

It really makes me proud to think that maybe I had a little something to do with the fact that Alyson made better choices when she left our school. I am so proud of how well she is doing, and I know that we will continue to keep in touch.

Teacher Story 2

When I first met Erin, she was hanging out with many of the kids in my classroom. She was one of my first students when I began teaching at FCEC.

Needless to say, I was overwhelmed with this job from the beginning and didn't really know what to expect. The students liked to see how much they could shock me with some of their statements, no matter how hard I tried to not show how surprised I was with some of the things they said.

I can remember walking down the hall, and I must have looked very unsure of myself because one of the high school students stated that they knew I was a new teacher and would probably be the first one to cry this year. It's funny now to think about this because I really didn't know what to expect. The first year was kind of tough, but I can't really imagine ever wanting to teach anywhere else. My job is so fulfilling because of the impact I hope to have had on some of the students.

Erin was in a rough home situation and went back and forth from mom to dad, not getting along with one or the other. I tried to listen to her and give what advice I could, but she was making some very bad choices about whom she was around after school. She came to our school after being caught with drugs that someone had put in her purse when they found out they were going to be searched. Even though she claims the drugs weren't hers, it didn't matter; she had possession and was sent to my school for a year.

Erin was a good student academically. The academics were never her problem. Erin's problems came from choices she made outside of school. After first semester, several of the students who had a negative influence on her were no longer at our school. She started making better choices about what she did after school, and her parents seemed to be more on the same page with how to handle things with her.

When Erin left our school to go back to her home school, I felt confident that she would do well. She and I always talked about how great it would be to go back to her home school and be able to hang out with her friends. She tried going to a different school, but it just didn't work for her. She went back to her original home school and did well her freshman year. She even came back to our school one day to "shadow" me for career day.

As we kept in touch, she told me things were going well—that is, until the day she called to tell me she was pregnant at 15. I was very surprised, to say the least. She told me that the father was a good guy and had finished high school and had a good job. They were getting married.

They did get married, but shortly after they were married, Erin had a miscarriage. Although she was disappointed, she knew that it was not the right time for her to have a baby. Erin is still married to the young man, and he works a full-time job. Erin has a part-time job and is a junior in high school now. She is doing well in school and seems to be doing better with her family. We keep in touch often, and I see her at her job (at a fast food restaurant).

She comes to school to visit sometimes and once brought her husband to meet me. She seems to be happy. I consider her one of our success stories even though she did get pregnant and married at such a young age; she has really done well by maintaining a job and staying in school and making good grades.

Teacher Story 3

Danny came to us as a freshman the very first year I started working at the Floyd County Education Center. Danny was the typical freshman. He had just left middle school and thought that high school would be as easy as middle school. Danny was a very bright student but did not apply himself in the classroom.

He was not a behavior problem but was very social, so it was difficult to keep him on task in the classroom. He struggled that semester to pass his math class, but he did it. He returned to his home school after his time at the FCEC. I would see him sometimes, and he would say that he was coming back. We hear that many times from former students because they like the small class sizes and the one-on-one attention that they receive at our school.

We also care very deeply about our students and their success when they return to their home school and when they go out into the real world. Luckily Danny was able to return to his home school and be successful, one of our goals at the FCEC.

In 2004, Danny sent me a letter at the school. He said that he was dating someone really nice and that he would be graduating in May 2004. He wanted to let me know he was graduating so that I would be there. When my students leave the school, I always tell them that I will be at graduation, and they remember. I also send them a card letting them know that I was there in case I do not get to see them at the actual graduation ceremony.

Danny complimented the entire Floyd County Education Center staff on helping him get back on the right path in life. He had made some bad decisions, but we were able to show him that one mistake does not have to ruin your entire life. I think that we made a difference in his life and his school success.

Fast-forward six years, and Danny is working and attending Georgia Northwestern Technical College. He is getting a degree in criminal justice. He is married and has a child. He owns his own home and has a lot of acreage to hunt and fish. For that he is very proud. His home situation was not the best, so he feels blessed to be able to have the American dream. His motto is "Live life to the fullest."

Teacher Story 4

A student had come over from a local county school for selling prescription pills on school property. He had surgery on his right hip and had been given pain medication to help in recovery. He sold a few of the pills to other students, for which he was eventually caught. School has many pressures and temptations, and for him this time was no different. He was athletic, polite, and respectful in my physical education class every day. However, he needed some work in the good decision category.

My classroom is an excellent platform to help many different types of students. One of my personal goals in teaching at my school is for me to establish common ground with each student. This allows me to build a good teacher-student relationship. I am able to get more out of my students when we have a healthy relationship.

For this young man, I used basketball and weights as a tool to get close to him. Through many private conversations I began to learn about his background and home situation. We worked on basketball and football skills mostly because of his interest to play sports in college. There were many talks about the decisions he had made up to this point and what he planned to do in the future.

Through the whole experience, he had realized how even small things can make a big difference in the path you will take in life. I explained to him that he could accomplish anything he wanted to if he would just set some short- and long-term goals and then commit to seeing them through. I wanted him to understand how others may try to derail him from his goals intentionally due to jealousy.

Success can separate people from even the closest of friends. Also peer pressure to have fun or do what is popular can be destructive and keep young people from staying committed to goals and dreams.

Today, he is back in his traditional school and doing very well. We, to this day, stay in touch regularly, and I continue to follow him through high school to help him with decisions and problems that may arise. I am also working with college recruiters on his behalf to assist him with college athletics. His grades are As and Bs, and he is doing the things necessary to make his dreams become reality.

With the right help and support, I believe he will definitely reach his goals and become a productive member in our society. You will never save them all, but it's the effort that matters. Students need someone to take an interest in them and who they are as a person. Don't judge the book by its cover, and be open to their needs. Prevention is much easier and an excellent way to keep students between the ditches.

REFLECTIONS FROM THE STUDENTS

Each student has the opportunity to reflect on his or her assignment in the nontraditional education program. Through surveys, essays, and interviews, the students are given the chance to share the experience and lessons learned at the FCEC. The following statements are taken from the information that has been collected. The 10 most common responses are given.

Question 1: What have been the strengths of attending alternative school?

- "My strengths have been that my attitude is changing. I'm not the same person I was then."
- "Some of the teachers have really taught me a lot about my anger and what to do with it. They have shown me I do have a brain. I just have to use it."
- "It has taught me respect and given me a whole other look at life."
- "Learning that I am not the only one out there with the same problems I have."
- "There are less people in the classrooms so you can have more individual attention when you need it and the teachers get to know me."
- "To learn a lesson from my negative behavior."
- "I've learned a lot! I have learned my lesson by improving my behavior and learning how to control my temper and anger issues."
- "Working hard, getting along with others, being nice, and meeting new people. Learning how to be respectful to people."
- "To help others through service learning. I never knew so many people need help in the community."
- "Caring people, quality staff with students as a priority."

Question 2: What has helped you the most at alternative school?

- "The levels on the Tier Factor. They make me act better and not want to get in trouble."
- "The one-on-one time with the teachers. I've got a lot of good grades when I really put my mind to it. The teachers that really have helped me showed that they wanted me to do well."
- "Staying out of trouble and away from drugs and that helping others isn't as bad as it seems."
- "The teachers and faculty at the school have helped me the most. They never stop pushing for more out of the students."

- "The fact that the teachers actually listen to you if you feel threatened or if you need help and other things of that nature."
- "The teachers never give up on you."
- "The teachers here have really talked to me and disciplined me for my actions; even though I may not like it, I've still learned from it."
- "Teachers working together to make us better and so we can have a better and brighter future."
- "Service learning."
- "All my teachers. They've played a big role in helping me graduate."

Question 3: Explain how the alternative school has or has not helped you become a better person.

- "It keeps me away from the drama, it helps me earn better grades, and I'm in a positive environment."
- "Well, I feel that it has taught me how to deal with certain situations like fighting. I can control myself better now, because I had nothing to lose when I got here and everything to gain, which I felt like made me a better person."
- "I know I am a better person because I am not making the same mistakes."
- "It taught me how to take responsibility for my action and how to take the good with the bad."
- "Alternative school has helped me become a better person by teaching me that life is shorter than you think and there's only one person that can make your life good or bad and that's yourself. The main thing it has taught me is respect."
- "It helped me to realize how much what I do affects the people I am closest to. I really do appreciate the alternative school for making me a better person."
- "The alternative school has taught me a lot more self-control."
- "It has helped me mature and to take responsibility for my actions."
- "It has helped me become a better person because now I can work in groups much better than I could before."
- "It has helped because I love people and teachers and helping others."

Realizing the need for everyone to work together is crucial for the learners to succeed. Taking the time to hear the voices of students and teachers shows the strategies have made an impact. The importance of empowering the learners to never give up on their dreams and goals goes hand-in-hand with the academic aspect in education. It shows how the nontraditional education program made a difference in the lives of students.

Conclusion

$\mathcal{T}$he strategies in this book are aimed at empowering youth at risk. This book is designed to refocus attention toward educating what is important in educating youth in today's society. Being intelligent is not necessarily being smart. Students are not robotic beings programmed to be shuffled through an assembly line of the education system only to perform well on tests. The products being shaped by schools are more than test scores; they are individuals with futures depending on their overall performance and choices.

Certain strategies in this book are research based according to education terminology; however, much of the approach comes from personal experiences of caring about students as individuals. The strategies provided throughout this book were designed to be different approaches to meet their needs in a different manner. Students who take ownership and an active role in their future create a greater motivation to succeed. Meeting them where they are and providing the necessary survival skills works with the right mindset of educators in a nontraditional educational setting or adults working with youth at risk.

You have seen examples of academic, behavioral, and social strategies for the youth at risk. The purpose of this book is to show readers:

- Students at risk learn differently from other students.
- Educating youth at risk is more than academics in the classroom. It requires a relationship based on caring for the students by helping them to meet basic needs to develop academically, behaviorally, and socially.
- Ideas and strategies to equip students with skills to become successful in whatever path they choose.

These have been done through the following approaches:

- Identifying techniques and strategies to empower at-risk students
- Sharing success stories of students who learned the importance of caring and developing life skills while improving academic achievement
- Showing successful strategies used by educators to provide ownership that enables success

No matter what variety of educational program is used to motivate students, the bottom line is that the people within the circle of influence are behind every effort the student faces. Our students are the future leaders, parents, workers, and citizens of our society. While tests and accountability are very important, the outcome is far greater than basing achievement on individual performance on tests. The information included in this book derives from educators who empower students to take ownership in their educational journey by using a variety of strategies and programs to meet the needs of the students.

The strategies target academic, behavioral, and social components in education. Each successful program has one common element that rises above anything else, and that is the element called empowerment! Building relationships is one of the main keys to success in school and every endeavor faced by the youth of our society. Success stories have shown how caring about the individuals has made a difference.

Education needs to refocus on the lives of the students. As mentioned earlier, accountability is important, and testing a crucial part of education; however, they are not the *only* parts that should be measured. True accountability would be to look at the students five years after completion of their chosen pathway and see where they fit in society. Are they productive members? Are they self-sufficient, reliable, and strong in work ethic?

We need to continue to develop strategies that will empower the students to become adults who make a difference in society. Listen to what the students are saying. Let each one buy into his or her trek toward success. Teach them the best way to learn and allow the world of digitization to be part of the process. Surround yourself with positive people who will support and help develop your dream. Most of all, remember that the students have hopes, dreams, and ambitions. They need you to help guide them and encourage them to be the best each one can be. Meet them where they are and set high expectations. Believe in the youth and challenge education to be the bright spot in the lives of the learners. Be the adult that each student will say played a significant role in influencing his or her life. Don't judge the success of the students, or the teaching, based on test results. These students are our future—they are *more than a test score!*

Appendix A

Weight Training Work-Out Chart

Weight Training Work-Out Chart

Name:				Block:		Date:	

Order	Muscle Area	Exercise	Training Load	Set	One	Two	Three
	Chest			WT.			
				Reps			
	Back			WT.			
				Reps			
	Shoulder			WT.			
				Reps			
	Arms (front of)			WT.			
				Reps			
	Arms (back of)			WT.			
				Reps			
	Abdomen			WT.			
				Reps			
				WT.			
				Reps			
				WT.			
				Reps			
				WT.			
				Reps			
				WT.			
				Reps			

Description of Active Warm-Up

Description of Cool-Down

Instructor Notes:

Appendix B

Project Planning Form

Project title:	**An Ounce of Prevention**
Teacher(s):	Melissa D. Martin
School:	Floyd County Education Center
Grade level(s):	9–12
Subjects:	Literature/Health/Technology

Standards-Focused
Project-Based Learning
Buck Institute for Education

Begin with the End in Mind

Summarize the theme for this project. Why do this project?

The theme for this project is "Many Reasons Why." Today's teen deals with many issues that often lead to teen depression. Students need to realize and reflect on how their actions and words can lead to teen depression and, in some cases, suicide.

Identify the content standard that students will learn in this project (two to three per subject).

ELARC4a—The student explores life experiences related to subject content area.
ELA_W1—The student produces technical writing that reports technical information and/or conveys ideas clearly, logically, and purposefully to a particularly audience.
ELWW3—The student uses research and technology to support writing.
ELA C2—The student produces legible work that shows accurate spelling and correct use of conventions of punctuation and capitalization.
ELA LSV1—The student participates in student-to-teacher, student-to-student, and group verbal interactions.

Identify key skills students will learn in this project. List only those skills you plan to assess (two to four per person).

1. **Communication**—crafting messages and using media effectively

2. **Collaboration**—cooperation, compromise, consensus, teambuilding, etc.

Identify the habits of mind that students will practice in this project (one to two per project).

1. **Listening to others with understanding and empathy**—monitor own thoughts while listening to someone else's ideas/words.

2. **Persisting**—sticking to a task until it is completed.

- *Does the project meet the criteria for standards-focused PBL?*

Craft the Driving Question

State the essential question or problem statement for the project. The statement should encompass all project content and outcomes and provide a central focus for student inquiry.

What factors contribute to teen depression and suicide in today's society?

• *Have you posed an authentic problem or significant question that engages students and requires core subject knowledge to solve or answer?*

Plan the Assessment

Step 1: Define the products for the project. What will you assess?

Early in the Project: Journals

Students will reflect each day on readings from *Thirteen Reasons Why*.

During the Project: Discussion on Paper Activity/Journals

Students will participate in a nonverbal activity called "Discussion on Paper." Students will silently move around and make comments on a quote, fact, or statement written out on a poster. Then students will participate in a verbal discussion of what was written.

Students will continue to reflect on each day's reading from *Thirteen Reasons Why*.

End of the Project: Student has choice of following:

1. Use media ranging from a 30-second radio/TV announcement, PowerPoint presentation, brochure, newspaper page, etc., to promote awareness about teen depression/suicide called "Got the Message?"

2. Create a proposal entitled "What Can Schools Do to Help Improve Students' Mental Health and Promote Awareness?" using choice of media: PowerPoint presentation, brochure, speech, etc.

Students must present end project to class.

Plan the Assessment (2)

Step 2: State the criteria for exemplary performance for each product.

Product: Journal

Criteria:

1. Student has entered a reflection from each day's reading from *Thirteen Reasons Why*.

2. Student has entered a reflection as directed by teacher about a statement, quote, or comment, etc.

Product: Proposal—"What Can Schools Do to Help Improve Students' Mental Health and Promote Awareness?"

Criteria:

1. Topic is specific.
2. Explains how their proposal will contribute to better mental health in the school community.
3. Explains why their proposal will contribute to better mental health in the school community.
4. Shows use of some type of media.
5. Meets high expectations in categories included in rubric of selected media.

Product: Media message—"Got the Message?"

Criteria:

1. Topic is about teen depression/suicide.
2. Media is used to promote awareness about teen depression/suicide to a wide audience.
3. Meets high expectations in categories in rubric of selected media.

Product:

Criteria:

• *Do the products and criteria align with the standards and outcomes for the project?*

Map the Project

What do students need to know and be able to do to complete the tasks successfully? How and when will they learn the necessary knowledge and skills? Look at one major product for the project and analyze the tasks necessary to produce a high-quality product.

Product: PowerPoint for Proposal/Message

Knowledge and Skills Needed	Already Have Learned	Taught Before the Project	Taught During the Project
1. How to create slides.	X		
2. How to import graphics.	X		X
3. How to transition slides.	X		X
4. How to add special effects.	X		X
5. How to add music.	X		X
6.			
7.			
8.			
9.			
10.			

What project tools will you use?
- ❑ **Know/need to know lists** ❑ _____
- ❑ Daily goal sheet ❑ _____
- ❑ Journals ❑ _____
- ❑ **Briefs** ❑ _____
- ❑ Task lists ❑ _____
- ❑ Problem logs ❑ _____

• *Do the products and tasks give all students the opportunity to demonstrate what they have learned?*

Map the Project (2)

List the key dates and important milestones for this project.

September 7: Start novel and journal reflections

September 13: Discussion on Paper activity/questions about novel

September 15: Start end project for presentations starting on 22nd

---

Use the Tuning Protocol with other teachers or a group of students to refine the project design or guide you further in your planning. What other thoughts do you now have on the project?

* *What challenges or problems might arise in this project?*

Manage the Process

List preparations necessary to address needs for differentiated instruction for ESL students, special-needs students, or students with diverse learning styles.

Diverse learning styles are already addressed in projects and group work.

Special-needs students include use of a paraprofessional for support, extended time, group work.

How will you and your students reflect on and evaluate the project?

Class discussion
Fishbowl
Student-facilitated formal debrief
Teacher-led formal debrief
Student-facilitated formal debrief
Individual evaluations
Group evaluations
Other: Journals

---

* *What do you expect to learn from this project?*

Appendix C

Project Planning Form

Project title:	**How Is Obesity More Than Just Being Overweight?**
Teacher(s):	Eric Burkhalter
School:	Floyd County Education Center
Grade level(s):	9–12
Subjects:	Health/PE

Standards-Focused
Project-Based Learning
Buck Institute for Education

Begin with the End in Mind

Summarize the theme for this project. Why do this project?

This project was created to investigate some of the areas that contribute to obesity and how our society classifies or views obese people.

Identify the content standard that students will learn in this project (two to three per subject).

#2—students will analyze the influence of family, peers, culture, media, technology, and other factors on health behavior (positive and negative influences).
#5—students will demonstrate the ability to use decision-making skills to enhance health (sustain healthy behaviors).
#3—students will demonstrate the ability to access valid information and products and services to enhance health (early detection and treatment).

Identify key skills students will learn in this project. List only those skills you plan to assess (two to four per person).

1. **Communication**—crafting messages and using media effectively

2. **Collaboration**—cooperation, compromise, consensus, teambuilding, etc.

Identify the habits of mind that students will practice in this project (one to two per project).

1. **Listening to others with understanding and empathy**—monitor own thoughts while listening to someone else's ideas/words.

2. **Persisting**—sticking to a task until it is completed.

• *Does the project meet the criteria for standards-focused PBL?*

Craft the Driving Question

State the essential question or problem statement for the project. The statement should encompass all project content and outcomes and provide a central focus for student inquiry.

How is obesity more than just being overweight?

• *Have you posed an authentic problem or significant question that engages students and requires core subject knowledge to solve or answer?*

Plan the Assessment

Step 1: Define the products for the project. What will you assess?

• Break down the parts of obesity that help answer the driving question.
• Research website creation and design.
• Brainstorm ideas on presentation and artwork themes.
• Narrow down topic

During the Project:
• Break down obesity through using the Internet.
• Gather data to support the topic.
• Discover ideas on how presentation should be displayed.

End of the Project: Student has choice of following:
• Complete website to demonstrate the culmination of data and design that was learned.
• Present website after completion to staff members.

Plan the Assessment (2)

Step 2: State the criteria for exemplary performance for each product.

Product: Outline

Criteria:
Students worked with instructor on how the project will be structured along with the content that it would possess.

Product: Draft

Criteria:
Should be well organized and show some direction for the common goal. Work was teacher directed.

Product: Edited drafts

Criteria:
Website with information was edited to ensure content and design was focused to support the driving question.

Product: Final version

Criteria:
Must be thoroughly checked for accuracy, design, and promotion of product. Students were excited and approved of the final website.

- *Do the products and criteria align with the standards and outcomes for the project?*

Map the Project

What do students need to know and be able to do to complete the tasks successfully? How and when will they learn the necessary knowledge and skills? Look at one major product for the project and analyze the tasks necessary to produce a high-quality product.

Product: PowerPoint for Proposal/Message

Knowledge and Skills Needed	Already Have Learned	Taught Before the Project	Taught During the Project
1. Organization			X
2. Development of project		X	X
3. Research methods	X		X
4. Design skills	X		X
5. Computer skills	X		X
6.			
7.			
8.			
9.			
10.			
11.			

What project tools will you use?

- ❏ **Know/need to know lists**
- ❏ **Goal sheet (what we want to accomplish)**
- ❏ Journals
- ❏ Briefs
- ❏ Task lists
- ❏ Problem logs

- ❏ <u>Brainstorming notes</u>
- ❏ <u>Notes and articles</u>
- ❏ <u>Research notes and articles</u>
- ❏ _____
- ❏ _____
- ❏ _____

- *Do the products and tasks give all students the opportunity to demonstrate what they have learned?*

Map the Project (2)

List the key dates and important milestones for this project.

Fall 2009: Organize topic and come up with a driving question. Create artwork and ideas for the obesity website.

Winter 2009: Begin research of topic and brainstorming to organize gathered information.

Winter/Spring 2010: Begin to create website with basic concepts and information (rough draft).

Spring 2010: Organize data and website to reflect the information obtained to answer the driving question.

April/May 2010: Complete website with many revisions to make sure everything looks good and supports the driving question.

Use the Tuning Protocol with other teachers or a group of students to refine the project design or guide you further in your planning. What other thoughts do you now have on the project?

Would have been easier if students would have remained at FCEC through entire project. Students returning back to their base schools and new students entering the class created a few hurdles. However, new students were brought up to speed quickly and did a good job in completing the project.

- *What challenges or problems might arise in this project?*

Manage the Process

List preparations necessary to address needs for differentiated instruction for ESL students, special-needs students, or students with diverse learning styles.

- Have computers available for students to use
- Allow student to contribute where their individual strengths can be served best
- Design and website creation
- Research skills
- Organization skills
- Presentation skills
- Allow students to work in the areas above where they can contribute

---

How will you and your students reflect on and evaluate the project?

Class discussion – small group or individual discussions
Fishbowl
Student-facilitated formal debrief
Teacher-led formal debrief
Student-facilitated formal debrief
Individual evaluations
Group evaluations
Other: <u>Journals</u>

- *What do you expect to learn from this project?*

Appendix D

Weekly Goal Sheet

Student _____ Week of _____

Directions: Each Monday you need to complete form for the week. This will enable you to keep up with assignments and progress. Turn in completed form before leaving class on Friday.

Monday, _____, 20 _____ Assignment(s) completed? YES   NO

Essential Question: _____

_____

Today I plan to complete the following assignments:

   1. _____

   2. _____

   3. _____

Tuesday, _____, 20 _____ Assignment(s) completed? YES   NO

Essential Question: _____

_____

Today I plan to complete the following assignments:

4. _____
_____
5. _____
_____
6. _____
_____

Wednesday, _____, 20 _____ Assignment(s) completed? YES NO

Essential Question: _____
_____

Today I plan to complete the following assignments:

7. _____
_____
8. _____
_____
9. _____
_____

Thursday, _____, 20 _____ Assignment(s) completed? YES NO

Essential Question: _____
_____

Today I plan to complete the following assignments:

10. _____
_____
11. _____
_____
12. _____
_____

Friday, _____, 20 _____ Assignment(s) completed? YES NO

Essential Question: _____
_____

Today I plan to complete the following assignments:

13. _____
_____

14. _____
_____

15. _____
_____

Appendix E

Student Goal Sheet

STUDENT GOAL SHEET

Physical Education

NAME:_____

Activities: Basketball

SPG = Student Participation Goal   S = Successful   Football
TPG = Teacher Participation Goal   N = Not Successful   Weights
ASPG = Actual Student Participation Goal   Ping Pong
                                                               Walking

SPG	Friday October 8th	TPG	Text Book
%	Goal:	90%	Other:
		S	
		N	
	Result:	ASPG	
	Teacher Comments:		

SPG	Friday October 22nd	TPG
%	Goal:	90%
		S
		N
	Result:	ASPG
	Teacher Comments:	

Appendix F

Student Sample Goal Sheet

STUDENT SAMPLE GOAL SHEET

Physical Education

NAME: <u>Sample Student</u>

SPG = Student Participation Goal
TPG = Teacher Participation Goal
ASPG = Actual Student Participation Goal

Activities:

S = Successful
N = Not Successful

Basketball   Ping-Pong
Football   Weights
Weights   Text book

Other:

SPG	Friday August 5th	TPG
90%	Goal:Increase my bench press max 5 pounds. Participate in class with good sportsmanshipsportsmanship.	90% S N
	Result: Received a 95 in participation but did not increase my bench press goal this week. Will try to improve the following week.	ASPG 95
	Teacher Comments: Student is working hard lifting weights. He reached his goal in cooperation and participation.	

→ Would circle "S" to indicate successful.

→ Student "SPG" was higher than expected.

SPG	Friday August 19th	TPG
85%	Goal: Beat my teacher at ping-pong who is the best in the school. Reach my participation target grade.	90% S N
	Result:I did not reach my participation target but I beat my teacher 1 out of 5 games in ping-pong. Still need to practice to get better.	ASPG 80
	Teacher Comments: Student did not participate one day.	

→ Would circle "N" to indicate not successful.

→ Student "SPG" was lower than expected.

Bibliography

Benard, B. (1991). *Fostering resiliency in kids: Protective factors in the family, school, and community*. Portland, OR: Northwest Regional Educational Laboratory.

Bluestein, Jane. (2001) *Creating emotionally safe schools: A guide for educators and parents*. Deerfield Beach, FL: Health Communications.

Brooks, J. G. (2004). To see beyond the lesson. *Educational Leadership, 62*(1), 8–13.

Cairncross, F. (2001). *The death of a distance: How the communications revolution is changing our lives*. Boston: Harvard Business School Press.

Chalker, C., and Stelsel, K. (2008). Mall schools: A new era for cutting edge alternative education. *International Journal on School Disaffection, 5*(2), 32–39.

Conway Middle School Student-Led Conferences. *Jefferson County Public Schools. Prichard Committee for Academic Excellence*. http://prichcom-cdn.s3.amazonaws.com/wp-content/uploads/2011/08/student-led_conferences.pdf.

Coyl, D. D., Jones, R. M., and Dick, A. J. (2004). The influence of peer status and peer relationships on school-related behaviors, attitudes, and intentions among alternative high school students. *American Secondary Education, 32*(2), 39–62.

Duckenfield, M., and Drew, S. (2006). *Growing to greatness*. St. Paul, MN: National Youth Leadership Council.

Edwards, M. A. (2001, May). One size doesn't fit all: Alternative schools and education programmes. *School Administrator, 58*, 36–39.

Friedman, M. I. (2005). *No school left behind: How to increase student achievement*. Columbia, SC: Institute for Evidence-Based Decision-Making in Education, Inc.

Hehir, T. (February 2007). Confronting ableism. *Educational Leadership, 64*(5), 8–14.

Lewis, A. C. (2006). Washington commentary: Clean up the test mess. *Phi Delta Kappa International, 87*(9).

Markham, Thom. (2003). *Project based learning*. 2nd ed. Novato, CA: Buck Institute for Education.

Martin, D. J. (2006). *Elementary science methods: A constructivist approach* (4th ed.). Belmont, CA: Thomson Wadsworth.

Milliken, B. (2007). *The last dropout: Stop the epidemic!* Carlsbad, CA: Hay House, Inc.

National Commission of Excellence in Education. (1983). *A nation at risk: The imperative for educational reform.* Washington, DC: U.S. Government Printing Office.

Nichols, S. L., and Berliner, D. C. (2008). Testing the joy out of learning. *Educational Leadership, 65*(6), 14–18.

Noddings, N. (2005). What does it mean to educate the whole child? *Educational Leadership, 63*(1), 8–13.

Popham, W. J. (2008, April). When the test says you're not so smart. *Educational Leadership, 65*(7), 87–88.

Prensky, M. (2008). Turning on the lights. *Educational Leadership, 65*(6), 40–45.

Slavin, R. E., and N. A. Madden. (1989). Effective classroom programs for students at risk. In R. E. Slavin, N. L. Karweit, and N. A. Madden (eds.), *Effective programs for students at risk.* Boston: Allyn and Bacon.

Smink, J., and Schargel, F. (2004) *Helping students graduate: A strategic approach to dropout prevention.* Poughkeepsie, NY: Eye on Education.

Strasburger, V. (2006). "Clueless": Why do pediatricians underestimate the media's influence on children and adolescents? *Pediatrics: Official Journal of the American Academy of Pediatrics, 117*(4), 1327–1431.

Swanson, C. B. (2003). Ten questions (and answers) about graduates, dropouts, and NCLB accountability. Brief number 3 in series *Learning curve: Facts and perspectives.* Washington, DC: Urban Institute, Education Policy Center.

Talevich, T. (2007, October). Stopping the dropout epidemic: How we can keep kids in schools and build a better future. *The Costco Connection*, 18–20.

Tapscott, Don. (1999). *Growing up digital: The rise of the net generation.* New York: McGraw-Hill.

Wilmes, D. J. (1995). *Parenting for prevention.* Minneapolis, MN: Johnson Institute.

About the Author

Melinda Strickland serves as the principal of the Floyd County Education Center. Currently in her 30th year of education within the Floyd County School System, Dr. Strickland began her teaching career as a middle school teacher at Armuchee Middle School and served as a varsity basketball coach at Armuchee High School. Past administrative positions included assistant principal for discipline at Model High School, Armuchee Middle School, and Armuchee High School, and as principal at Model Middle School.

CPSIA information can be obtained at www.ICGtesting.com
Printed in the USA
BVOW08s0748251013

334602BV00003B/9/P